THE NEPHIAD

Borgo Press Books by MICHAEL R. COLLINGS

All Calm, All Bright: Christmas Offerings
The Art and Craft of Poetry: Twenty Exercises Toward Mastery
Brian Aldiss
Dark Transformations: Deadly Visions of Change
The Films of Stephen King
GemLore: An Introduction to Precious and Semi-Precious Gemstones
The House Beyond the Hill: A Novel of Horror
In the Void: Poems of Science Fiction, Myth and Fantasy, & Horror
The Many Facets of Stephen King
Naked to the Sun: Dark Visions of Apocalypse
The Nephiad: An Epic Poem in XII Books
Piers Anthony
Scaring Us to Death: The Impact of Stephen King on Popular Culture
Singer of Lies: A Science Fantasy Novel
Wordsmith, Part One: The Veil of Heaven: A Science Fantasy Novel
Wordsmith, Part Two: The Thousand Eyes of Flame: A Science Fantasy Novel

THE NEPHIAD

AN EPIC POEM IN XII BOOKS

by

Michael R. Collings

Emeritus Professor of English
Seaver College
Pepperdine University

THE BORGO PRESS
An Imprint of Wildside Press LLC

MMX

Borgo Laureate Series
ISSN 1082-3336

Number Four

Copyright © 1996, 2010 by Michael R. Collings

All rights reserved.
No part of this book may be reproduced in any form
without the expressed written consent
of the author and publisher.

www.wildsidebooks.com

FIRST WILDSIDE EDITION

CONTENTS

Book I 9
Book II 25
Book III 39
Book IV 53
Book V 68
Book VI 85
Book VII 99
Book VIII 113
Book IX 134
Book X 147
Book XI 161
Book XII 181

Afterword 198

About the Author 201

THE NEPHIAD

BOOK I

The Author provides a Prologue in which the Prophetic Role of Milton is defined and Milton's relationship to the Prophet of the Restoration, Joseph Smith, and the Book of Mormon *considered; The Author invokes Urania, the Holy Spirit, as his Muse; Nephi, youngest son of Lehi, is found in Prayer upon a Mount; The Lord reveals to Nephi promises of future blessings and greatness contingent upon obedience; The youth returns to his father's camp.*

OF Man's first disobedience and consequence
For earth-born Sons and Daughters of our fallen
God-sired Parents' sin, need *none* more speak;
One greater far than any modern Bard
Gave voice to truths inspired by the Holy
One addressed through Epic Voice upraised;
In poverty, in anguish for his Cause,
In Darkness absolute, from sightless Orbs
He peered forth in endless magnitude
Of human intellect, to see unseeing
High Eternal Truths of God's great Plan
Emanating from Celestial Thrones
To lighten all God's Children's myriad souls;
For hearts and minds to him now subsequent,
Who through long generations read his words
And felt instinctively their native Truth—
For these did *Milton* frame his Epic Tale,
For these he spoke with accents ponderous,
With Voice proclaiming from blind Darkness' depths

As one within the arid wilderness
Of Judah's land; not camel's armor rude
Nor stark diet of locust and sweet honey
From wild Deseret for him—to one
Than whom of woman born none greater was
Was given *that* glorious Call: *"Prepare the way*
For God, make straight a desert Highway for
The King!" To one was given true, high Power
To usher in *Messiah,* Reign of Peace,
To one of woman born, of priestly lines
Through *Zacharias* and *Elizabeth*
In their great age and barrenness; to him
Named *John Baptizer* did the Call descend
To be forerunner to the Promised Lamb.
Nay, it was not this John of latter days
Who preached th'Eternal Gospel of rebirth;
Instead, on him was placed the task divine
To serve as one of many, forge from old
A world renewed, a World receptive to
The Reëstablishment of Truths embodied
In the ONE by Zacharias' Son
High-testified. An English *John*, removed
From his progenitor by the ignorance
And leaden still of sixteen times the span
Of centuries; another John, inspired
By Him on High, preparing worlds for him
Who was to come, Joseph's son, of whom
The ancient *Nephites* spoke, who was to come
Before the bright Millennial Day should dawn
In purple, sky-inspiring Majesty,
That to his common, humble patronym
High honors might accrue and praising notes
Unto a living Prophet of the Lord.
Yea, ere the Prophet Joseph drew first breath,
Before his grandsire looked upon Earth's skies,
Another John approached eternal Truth
And built beneath the arching Canopy

Of False Assumption an Edifice divine,
Sacred Shrine to Truth, a Poem sublime;
Not perfect, no! but perfect more by far
Than erring Creeds of men's Theologies.
    A Voice of Truth, speaking to our Day,
A Voice emerged from dusts of Ages past;
Branded as heretical by men
And by wise scholars learned who understood
But poorly workings of the Holy One
In guiding and inspiring Chosen Seers,
Revealing Truths for ages lost to men;
A Voice inspired, but lacking right and claim
To that prophetic honor borne of old
By servants of the Most High God, from Adam—
Hero strong and resolute, whose Son
Fulfilled the just commands of Highest Heaven,
Exchanging Eden for a world of growth,
A world of Transitory happiness,
Men leading through high Justice's firm Decrees,
Subservient to Mercy's Holy Grace,
To worlds above our mundane, human Sphere
In which we could in truth be as the Gods
Through true obedience to laws divine—
To *Christ*, the Son, the King, greater than
All others; in Himself the Giver and
Fulfiller of all Law. No, inspired
Though he be, no Prophet; for himself
And him alone—in his sole name—could Cromwell's
Blinded, brilliant scholar chant his hymn
To God's Eternal Plan—to Justice through
The Father, Mercy through th'Anointed Son.
In his sole name—for not through all the Ages
Gave there men to speak *for* God—not since
John, the Loved Apostle of the Lord
Wrote his last from dismal Patmos' Isle
And joined the other three whose names no soul
Yet knows—or at the least reveals—in filling

In the flesh our Lord's express Commands:
Mortal immortality, undying
life, until pale Death's pale power by Him
Is overcome—yea, not since John had Western
Lands heard Prophets' voices pronounce with force
And Heaven's mighty Power: *'The Lord hath said!*
Thus speaks the Lord of Heaven and of Earth!'
The need remained, for always gave and will
The Word of God for all frail flesh full answers
Give to fundamental hopes and queries
Growing from the mortal depths of Soul.
The need remained, but Worthiness and Faith
Declined; Almighty *God* replaced, supplanted
By crude-carven notions false, by Gods of men
Which had no power to see, to hear, to eat,
To smell; possessing neither body, parts,
Nor passions; no, not Gods! mild shadows merely
Of the Substance of perfected Being.
All true hope and Knowledge of God's Laws
And Truths were lost, distorted throughout Time.
    Darkness, silence, the Voice and Light of God
No more among the Earth-bound progeny
Of parent stock from Eden's Garden scourged;
A famine, not of grain nor drink, but of
The Word and Will of God revealed. Yet some
Perceived the first pale tints of breaking Dawn,
The Promise of the Day and knowledge high;
Some, as *Milton*, whose bright intellect
Dispersed the veil of Ignorance to peer
Into deep truths by men and creeds obscured;
Or some, as great *Traherne*, dead in the year
Of Milton's death though still young in greatness
And imaginative power, whose Visions
Of a Childhood close to God in memory,
Of Memories of a Pre-Life nearest God,
Suffused the harvest splendor of his words,
His *Centuries* that over centuries

All nigh to disappeared from human view,
His Gospel of *Felicitie* unheard;
Or others, as aged *Wordsworth*, in the Island
Realm, who knew, through intimation's Light, things
Before mortality, who in a Time
Of meditative calm, a Season of
Calm Weather, distant breakers heard of Seas
Celestial, perceived our prior state,
Revealed our trailing Glory-Clouds to all;
Thus to the Poets, *Vates*, came the gleam
Of Hesperus, Morning Star divine,
To hail the Coming Light, the Coming Son;
But this to few—for most, the Heaven's Son,
Once set, would and should no more upon
This Earth appear. Most took no thought to ask
Of God for truths by sons of men defiled,
By God removed from sin-filled Earth's dominion—
Most took no thought until that Morn in Spring;
Young *Joseph* in a Holy Grove down-knelt
And asked, and in return received, from God
A Revelation most supremely true.
His History speaks, and we need no more say:
Joseph, true to Prophet's Holy Call,
Fulfilled the Law and sealed with *Martyr*'s Blood
His witness to high Truths. Building firmly,
Using rocks and stones amassed by these,
Earlier men of inspiration, he
Restored, revealed, and reëstablished here,
In Latter Days he reëstablished here
On Earth, the *Church of Jesus Christ*, our Lord.
    And thus, O Milton, we, the Children of
Those Latter Days, owe you and countless lesser
Ones our thanks; you carved the way for God;
Toiled to set the bedding stones for desert
Ways, prepared the path for Prophecies
And Prophets to reveal the Will of God.
You opened up the minds of men to Truth,

And burst the Darkness with your brilliant flash
Of Inspiration and of Godly Hope;
And now, in worlds of Life and Growth unseen,
In flaming presence of that Holy One
Whose earthly mission you perceived and knew
As few before, as few for all the years
'Twixt John and you, 'twixt you and Joseph's son'
Yea, now, in presence pure of Heaven's Son
You know the Truth—Eternal, perfect All,
Taught to those who could not see for seeing,
Who could not hear because they heard too much,
Who did not know, condemned by wiles, deceit,
And falsehood rife among the fall'n of Men.
In this great host of waiting Human Souls
Have you now seen, and heard, and understood
Who once in Darkness sought the Light of Life
To justify the Ways of God to Men.
    From your mind inspired poured forth your tale,
Great Visions of a Paradise profaned,
The founding of the Human Race on Earth,
And intimations of the Coming Lord,
The Son, whose rising should eclipse the Sun,
And at whose setting all the Earth in sable
Drapery bedecked for mourning hours
Should mourn. To equal your deft power of words
I dare not hope; to equal prove to your
Celestial subject's scope I dare not try.
And therefore for the object of my Pen
I choose a lesser man than Father Adam,
A man heroic, praised in *Joseph*'s Book,
Praised in *Mormon*'s Chronicle of Gold,
An ancient Prophet, Warrior of his God,
Who placed his Faith upon the Lord's Commands
And thus became a Savior to his Folk,
And to all flesh to whom his words should come;
Lesser, true, than he. the First of Men,
Whose name itself, like he, was formed from *Earth*;

But strong in his own right, a valiant youth
Who broke a high command to obey God;
No private but a person raised to powers
From Heaven lent to save his Father's line.
    Of heroes hidden long by Earth's gray dust,
Of nations long to men unknown I sing;
Of nations led by Israel's God into
A Western *Paradise*, scant years before
The tyranny of Babylon destroyed
God's templed City fair; of brothers' ire
Against a righteous youth, poisoning
With hatred's venomous edge generations
Of their progeny; of men both fair
And dark; of the Spirit's awesome power,
Manifest through *Nephi*'s courage high;
To write of these I set my humble pen,
But not of all; for prophets long ago
Have written full accounts upon bright metal
Plates by Joseph's diligence brought forth,
By Nephi's faith attained for Lehi's seed.
Nay, I intend but partial tale to tell,
An episode, important in itself,
And in its implications for my day;
For in this single Act is all contained
That *Mormon*'s golden-throated words relate,
The means by which a Chosen Race of God
Preservéd was from Ignorance and Death
Through actions more than martial by a youth
Performed, a youth in years though not in form,
Who Fortitude of Soul exhibited,
Great Strength in serving high, divine Desires,
Great Wisdom in discerning Heaven's Desires.
Thus Milton's mighty Muse I now invoke
Who guided him in his most Christian Tale:
Thou, Holy One, Thou Comforter, whose role
It is to testify and bring to all
Remembrance of things past; Thou Spirit, Thou,

Who freed young Joseph from fiendish bands
As he in faithful prayer inquired of God
For Knowledge and for Truth; Thou Spirit, Thou,
Who fills creative Souls with Truth's pure Powers,
To Thee I pray in eager expectation
For aid and strength and wisdom in my Task.
    As at the Earth's beginning, primal Day,
When *Chaos*'s ancient reign was seized by Him
Who is the Universal Arbiter
And source of Truth and never-failing Form;
When from th'Abyss a World appeared in space
As God's creative Spirit moved across the Deep,
Enshrouded in the cloakéd mists of Dark,
Until, through generative powers unleashed,
That Light which is the Glory of the Father
And the Son—that Son Who is the Glory
Of the Father's Light—burst in flashing arcs
To dissipate vile sway of Night
And icy Void, and to divide with force
The warring Elements; so at the Dawn,
Remembrance of created Time's first state,
Earth rolls upon her axis through th'Æther
Of the universe, disclosing to
The constant, wheeling Eye of brilliant Day
Deep-hidden secrets of her night-veiled round;
The Westward march of Heaven's golden fire,
Reflecting first from mountainous eminence,
Soon kindles sparkling splendors in that Sea
Which split asunder at soft touch of Moses'
Staff, when Walls of upreared, watery glass
Proved allies to swift-fleeing Promised Ones,
Israel's progeny, *Egypt*'s suffering slaves,
In their long-awaited, harried Exodus
From tyranny and tyrants' graven gods;
Holding back wild, storm-whipped, surging seas,
High sentient waves permitted slaves to pass,
Then shattered as *Busiris* and his

Memphian chivalry with glistening arms
Pursuing closely hegiratic hosts
Rode pridefully across the drying beds—
To drown as Nature's torrent-flows unbound
And baptized dusky Egypt unto Death.
Then stood the sons of Goshen on bare shores,
Beneath the arm protective of that man
Whose might confounded priestcraft's pagan charms,
And witnessed thus the Power of their God—
The floating carcasses and shattered wheels,
Thick bestrewn upon the waves, were as
Deep-fallen Ones by Milton sung, who sprawled
Abject and lost upon dark-flaming seas
Of Hell until by their tyrannic King
Upraised to greater infamy and man's
Destruction hoped for and in part achieved;
Or were as drowning beasts and men when Heaven
In anguish for base's wickedness first op'd
The fountains of the opal sky and wept
Upon the Earth, that only few were saved
Alive to propagate the race: mild son
Of him who first brought fire, *Deucalion*,
And his make, *Pyrrha*; or th'ancient man who dwelt
Beyond the Mountains of the Sun, whose name
Reported is in *Gilgamesh*'s tale
Of search for immortality by man,
Utnapishtim, ancient one and serpent-foe,
Keeper of grave secrets, secret graves—
Both of whom were but brief shadows of
The son of *Lamech*'s eld, whose vessel huge
Preserved alive all species in the Earth
When God rained down tear-floods to cleanse this globe.
    Daily through slow-marching Centuries
From *Sinai*'s Shepherd to the Monarchy
Of *David*'s House and blessed Seed, beyond
To threatened Conquest at Oppressor's hands
And second Fall into Captivity,

The new-born Daylight swept red-shadowed floors
And desert wastes surrounding reed-edged Seas
That witnessed Moses' powers; hillocky sands
Glowed fresh in dewy morn, and Palm oases
Starkly stood above their shadowed selves;
Beneath their fronded crests a freshet flowed
Into salt sea-waves' unrestraining forms,
emerging from its sheltering vale to join
Its waters with cool fountains from the Deep.
Ancient and immovable this vale
That bears sweet, living waters at its heart;
Through it once passed life's joyous tread
As Israel *Nilotic* bonds threw off
And sought again her Fathers' lands;
Now here again a fleeing band appeared,
Found sustenance and rest upon green shores
Of sea and stream—a prophet's family,
Who feared not centuries of slavery past
But rather future, devastating Wars.

  Beneath the Palms, beside the streamlet's song,
The curéd hides of animals formed tents,
Desert homes for waiting wanderers,
Exiles from *Judæa*'s luxuries.
And now, as morning Light first gilded sands,
Toward red-dawning East, one figure moved.
In silence; across smooth, wind-worn desert stones
He walked toward morn's Solitude of Light,
Soon leaving far behind the shelt'ring tents.
Alone, unarmed, yet without fear of hurt,
Unconscious of the power of beasts to hurt,
Unobserved into waste wilderness
The youngest son of four (of stature large,
In frame well-grown) traversed the valley's floor
Toward white Light that signified his God.

  Bold *Nephi*, in the Desert Dawning, walked
With eyes downcast, intent on infant thoughts
(*Wordless* thoughts that struggled to find Words),

Upon the coruscating, sandy trail
That led toward the sacred Mount nearby;
An ancient mound of weathered, rocky mien,
Ripped erst from Earth's foundation-beds when Time
Began—and History—with Adam's tread
Behind high, verdant walls of *Paradise,*
Or so it seemed, so hoar with massive age
And lithified antiquity the Mount
There stood, anointed with pure, holy Dews
Of Dawn, its crest a golden, glowing Crown
Set on its brow by Nature's sovereign Lord.
Few moments passed before the steadfast tread
Of him who thus pursued his lonely way
Across wide stretches to the Mountain's flank
Attained sere heights that overlooked the land;
Harsh, treeless heights, no banks of spicy herbs
Or beds of flowerlets wild to scent the air
With moistures odoriferous and cool—
Pungent, perfumed, with honeys rife, and cool—,
But blasts of heated breath from Eastward blown
Spilling over the Mount to boil across
Far-stretched immensities of Moses' Sea;
Upon this barrenness no growth endured,
Only stony jewels sparkled on
This highest eminence; and here before
A rudimentary altar by himself
Once formed, the youth in prayer down-knelt unto
His God, to plead for softened hearts and faith
In Dreams and Visions by his father seen;
Before his altar, mighty Nephi knelt,
Young in years, in flesh exceeding strong,
Desirous of obtaining through his prayers
Sure knowledge of High Mysteries of God
Vouchsafed through *Angel*'s presence to his Sire
Visionary *Lehi*, in the City
Of the Shepherd-Kings. Before his altar
He raised high strong arms unto the Lord,

Cried with soul-delved strength unto his Lord;
Until to him in Dawning calm a Voice
Descended from Celestial Courts above
All realms of middle-air, from whence proceed
As from the Mouth of God those mandates high
That govern Universal Harmonies
Since first and long before our Earth's green spark
Assumed its place within the Firmament;
From Kolob's majesty, the Seat of God,
In near propinquity to Solar Flames
(Whose light is to their God's as *Stygian* black
Is to the fire omnipotent of Noon);
From that great Planet wheeling at the Core
Of all Creation came a Voice Divine
To Nephi's waiting heart, and to him thus,
As if in Council grave assembled were
All Hosts of Heaven's crystal Spheres to hear
Words' passage from the Lord of All to man,
To hear the counsel of their mighty King
Expressed in chosen terms to Lehi's son:
    "Nephi, Son and wanderer in my Cause,
Blessed thou art and blessèd yet to be;
For *I am God*, and thou in purest Faith
Hast sought to hear and know my Words and Will
Unto the race of Adam's progeny.
Diligently hast thou sought for me, my Son,
With heart compressed in low Humility;
And inasmuch as thou shalt keep those Laws
Which shall be given of me—and are—behold,
Thy Cause shall prosper through my *Name*, and thou
Shalt flourish as the Rose of Paradise
Within a Land of Promise granted thee;
Yea, even such a land as I shall form,
Prepare for chosen, fertile seed; a Land
Which choice above all other Nations stands,
Where thou shalt dwell, together with the sons
Unto thy Brethren born, through many years,

Until I in my wisdom shall send forth
From shores within the spheres of Judah's power
Brave mariners, into whose hearts I shall
Deep urges place, that they seek out thy line
And thee again to history's path make known.
This I promise—and pleasure's joys replete—
To all obedient Souls who love my Word,
To all endearing Souls who hear my Word;
But those who flaunt themselves against thy word
And seek unjust dominion o'er themselves
As noxious weeds and thistles shall be burned,
By their own stubbornness and sinful pride
Severed from the presence of their Lord!
For thou, my Son, if thou in Righteousness
Submit thy will to Heaven's divine Decrees,
Obedience exhibit in thy works,
As Ruler sovereign o'er thy People set
To guide their lives within the Promised Land
Shalt thou ordainéd be, and set apart
To function as preceptor to my Folk'
Not as Mystagogue, to initiate
This People into Darkness and Deceit,
Into Rites and Rituals displeasing
To thy God; but rather as a mentor
In my Gospel's clarity. And behold,
This more I promise thee, that thou above
All other seed of Lehi's loins are blessed
Because of thy humility and love,
And I have thee anointed as a King;
As *Samuel* once pondered *Jesse*'s line
Before he with pure oil consecrate
Sweet *David*, youngling of the Flock, endowed,
So I anoint thee now as Priest and King,
This right is thine, through my Authority;
And now I say, thy Brethren shall be warned
That in the day that they through conscious Act
Rebel against thee and thy Rule decreed,

And thereby move against express commands
And grave Authority of God dispensed
By me, through mine own Words conferred on thee,
In that day, in that hour, do I pronounce
Them curst, maladict, through their own choice,
To woe and weary fears subservient;
Cursed shall be their seed, and in their line
Shall all civility be lost, except
It be that they repent and come to me
Through thee and through thy ministering voice.
    "Thus stands immutable my Law confirmed,
Estábishéd as Earth's foundations first
From pre-existing Elements were formed
By *Elohim*'s desire, and by the Force,
The motive Force of great *Jehovah*'s Voice;
And power o'er thee and o'er thy Seed shall not
Devolve to them, so long as thy Seed stands
Immutable in their obedience,
Devoted to thy word and to their God;
But if it be that they, thy Seed, do rise
In wickedness and gross iniquity
And vaunt their Strength as men above their God's,
Then shall thy Brethren's Seed be to thine own
A scourge, a whip of thorns, afflictions to
Frail flesh, to bring them once again unto
Remembrance of their covenants with me,
Their God, the God of Israel, and of
All Worlds and Times throughout Eternity;
And if they bring not forth repentant fruits,
If they, thy Seed, bow not with contrite heart
Before their God, their Brethren's Seed shall wars
Employ and battles wage, that none survive
To blot the Promised Land with sin-stained tread;
Yet pray and hope, my son, and strive thy best
This wretched Fate through patient Faith to change."
    Thus spake the Immortal One from His Eternal Throne
Unto a son of man as he, the man,

In attitude of Prayer bowed upon
A Mountain desolate in desert Wastes
And strove for Wisdom, Strength, and Knowledge high,
Understanding and a godly Patience
In dealing with recalcitrant brethren
Who would not walk within the ways of God
Nor heed the urgent warnings of their aged
And weary Father as he revealed to them
The dictates of the Holy One above.
    Long moments Nephi knelt upon cool sands,
Statue-like, as if upon the plains
Of Israel the ancient pagan Myths
Of Gods were true, and he the victim sore,
Stone-transfixed, of her whose snaky locks
And brazen claws struck terror in the
Craven heart of *Polydictes* King,
Until *Danae*'s heroic son, by *Zeus*
Begot in golden shower, from wise *Athene*
Armed with mirrored shield of gold, by *Hermes*'
Wingéd sandals fleet-endowed with more
Than mortal speed, celerity of gods,
With savage thrust of sword, directed by
Dread image in the shield, severed quite
The vip'rous *Gorgon*'s sleeping head, from whence
Upon the shield by Wisdom's goddess borne,
The monstrous head affixéd firmly was
To turn into congealéd stone all foes
Who dared to bend their eyes toward that sight;
Thus Nephi stone-like stayed—and yet not so,
For as wild Gorgon horrors manifest
Were, pagan powers impressed upon each form,
Each lithic form, and faces long retained
Their twisted visages of fear until
Erased by Time's erosive hand and thus
Released unto oblivious peacefulness;
Nay! not so were Nephi's lineaments
Which etched effusive awe and joy into

His heart, which mirrored glories of High Sights
Celestial—he knelt, until impelled
By inner Voice to rise, he followed paths
From Mountain top to Desert floor, returned
Unto the tents of Lehi's caravan,
Retreated ere the withering heat of Day
With all-consuming Fires upon the Mount
Descended as the Presence of the Lord,
As if the living Presence of the Lord
Were come as once to Sinai's towering heights;
Yea, Nephi rose, and strode with youthful grace
Unto the gracious shade of Lehi's tents
Unto the shade of aging Lehi's tents.

BOOK II

Laman and Lemuel, Nephi's elder brethren, are introduced, murmuring and complaining against their Father and his Dreams; They desire to return to the wealth and ease they once enjoyed in Jerusalem; Sam, the third brother, approaches to bring his brothers to Lehi's tent, where their father, in great anxiousness of mind, desires to speak unto his sons; Lehi commissions his sons to return to Jerusalem to acquire the Plates of Brass.

As one returned from Sweet Communion with
His Father's God, two brothers stirred and stretched,
Two elder sons of Lehi Patriarch,
Who seemed in their perversity and guile
As two from *Pandæmonium* emerged,
Base *Pandæmonium*, exultant seat
Of Hell's unjust, despotic Monarchy
In all its Orient panoply of
Jeweled streets and high-enameled Walls;
As two subaltern dæmons fall'n with Pride
Beneath infernal sway of *Satan*'s wiles
Supported vaunting Lucifer's low schemes,
Participated with Hell's murmuring *Crew*—
Moloch Homicide, rebellion's God,
Rebellion's King against the Powers of Heaven,
His woeful rage upraising, pitiable rage,
That thought to mount the highest Throne of God,
As sceptered King and Lord o'er Heaven's Domains;
Or *Mammon Sybarite,* pleasure's low King,

Who strove an imitative Heav'n to raise
Within the murky Realm of black-flamed Hell,
Whose thoughts entire on wines luxurious dwelt,
On pleasure's fantasies and slothful ease—
As these Infernal Councilors, who once
With Morning's Fallen Star conspired Man's Fall,
(Or thought, not knowing *Satan*'s Policy,
Beëlzebub's matching Policy,
Both fraudulent and without final hope),
So seemed the brethren twain who now awoke;
With heavy yawns replacing Orisons,
The elder pair of Lehi's sons awoke
To face the day with murmurings and plaints
Against their agéd father and his God.

  Dawn was far spent as first the two emerged
From cooling, golden-shady bowels of
Thick, cave-like tents to sit in indolence
Beneath green-crested Palms and thus converse,
First the elder to the second, eldest
Laman spoke unto his brother: "Dreams! Dreams!
Because of foolish dreams we languish in
This filthy, wearing waste of desert drear;
We, whose treasure-house encrustéd heaps
With gold and precious stones and carven wood,
Silver plates and ewers finely wrought;
Whose limbs till now but bore smooth, liquid lengths
Of fair and costly Oriental silks;
Now, behold! beneath this burning sun
We sit, all meanly clad in stiffened skins
With but a native roof and earthen floor.
Because of him as exiles we must roam
Through this accurséd waste. And why? Yea, why?
Foolish dreams of an agéd, senile mind!"

  He whose bitter thoughts thus access found
In futile words to curse his fallen lot
With gesture savage turned his back from him
Who now proposed rejoinder to the first,

From *Lemuel*, second son, who touched dry tongue
To drier lips and spake with voice low-pitched,
With tones as glossed as softly polished gold:
"The feasts—ah, Laman! can you not still taste
And savor through this choking dust high joys
Relished once in good Jerusalem?
The wines and fruits—sweet dates, sweeter peaches,
Melons, apricots—with icy chill prepared,
Celebratory viands for a king,
The new-anointed *Zedekiah* King,
Whose coronation feasts outshone in glory,
Wealth, and splendor all which came before.
Even now in *David*'s City, streets
Must sound with joys and joyous revelry
To the King; rose-crowned banqueters
Feasting in the Golden Hall of Kings
Within the palace of great *David*'s line
Must share tart dainties delicate and light,
Such as tongues of *Eber* rarely taste;
And dark-eyed beauties, fresh and youthful blooms,
Grow yet unplucked, their rose of loveliness
Not yet inwoven in a Crown of Love,
To grace the fronting brow of some fair youth,
Unfolds smooth petals to rich morning Dews,
Now glows as pink-hued petals in the light
Of dewy morn. O brother Laman, those
The joys we left behind to turn our faces
Toward dull desert fastnesses, when we,
As heirs of Israel's might stock, should live
According to the stature we deserve."
    To whom the first with raging accents thick
Rejoined, in passion's powers entrancéd held:
"Thus should we, brother, of such luxuries
Partake, instead of scorching under skies
As dead and faded as a leaden pall,
Beneath those heav'ns whose too-near touch brings death
From parching, searing thirst, or at the least

Destroys the mind with fever-throbbing fear,
Save for nomadic sons of *Ishmael*,
Whom centuries of harshness have inured
To desert ways, coarsened to desert life;
These with near imperviousness oft move
Great households o'er gray, shifting, sullen sands
As if straight paths were truly marked and held;
And we, true Chosen Sons of Israel's wealth
And rich inheritance, squat by Palms
To eat tough, uncooked, bitter flesh of beasts,
To share unserving exile with those few
Who choose to follow where a madman's dreams
Might lead, as if we shared communal guilt
With that sin-laden beast which yearly toils
Beneath th'unaccustomed burden of
Men's guilt, and into thirst-pinched Arabah
Is scourged, to meet with waiting *Azazel*
And thus Atonement make vicariously,
Erewhile its sacred counterpart is slain
By *Aaron*'s hand to expiate God's Wrath
Within the hush-veiled Holy Place of Fire;
Yea, we true Sons of God's Magnificence
Must leave behind our treasures stored and bound
And treasures more in jewelry, food, in gold,
And in those crownets fresh of female charms
That never now will ornament our brows
To signify a Conquest and Reward!"
    Thus brother unto brother spake, while wrath
As flames of *Hephæstus*' Fires sparked
In eyes deep-set beneath thick, swarthy brows
Of Lehi's sons; and thus grim ire burst forth
Impatient and obsessed, as spake two men—
Yea, men in body and in strength of will,
Yet callow youths in understanding Truths
Beyond mere pleasures base of sense-desires
Or pleasing powers of prideful Might unjust
Wielded o'er long-suffering servitors—

So sounded through still desert air their words,
Replete with memories of luxuries
And joys in sweet Jerusalem. And as
They spake, these sons uncompromised of wealth
Amassed, abandoned, to them came a third,
Unto these brethren twain the third drew nigh
Of four, young *Sam*, whose bearded face bore proof
Of guileless youth and high nobility,
Younger than these two yet not the youngest
Son now dwelling in great Lehi's desert tents..
With bitter taunts his elder brethren called,
Responding to the younger's hailing voice
As he them sought with calm and warming tones.
Thus Laman to his brother Lemuel
With smile sardonic spake: "And now, behold,
Where comes our brother Sam, the little one,
To chide us with the example of his youth
And righteousness, the wisdom of his beard
But newly grown. Another Nephi, he,
As Nephi is, no scion true exposed
Of Israel's parent stock, but false engrafted
They, who honor not traditions of our
Past, our glories, and our victories;
Our little brother comes with sniveling voice
To make more miserable desert loneliness.
Here, little one, what would you now of us?"

    With somber tread the third of Lehi's sons
Approached, lowly greeting Laman and
Dark Lemuel with words of grace and joy;
"Brothers, may the God of Israel's past,
Of *Abraham*, of *Isaac*, and your own
With His Beneficence upon you smile
This brilliant morn; for now I bring request
That you repair with me unto the tent
Which shelters Lehi from harsh desert heat
And desiccating winds. I urge you, haste!
For he in great excitement calls for you,

That he unto his sons this morn might speak."
    He spake, and to him answered Lemuel,
His eyes quick-darting to dark Laman's face,
As if there seeking approbation's glint:
"No doubt another dream invaded has his mind;
Perhaps he has received God's word that we
Unto white-lotus-bordered, flooding *Nile*,
To *Pharaoh*'s gilded Court in Memphian might
And majesty should go, to preach as *Aaron*
And his brother did, to call upon
Grim, heathen priests the livid judgments of
An angry, jealous God. Perhaps we, too,
Shall touch the water's brown with white-ash staves
And see green waves obey our fevered will,
Till we—dry-shod—shall pass beyond this camp,
This desolation sere of heat and thirst,
This drear abomination of sharp sands,
Unto our own oft-Promised Land of wealth
Where we beneath God's warming smile shall rest."
    Then Laman interruptive raised on high
His plaining tongue to speak: "More hopeful still,
More probably, perhaps our mother's hand
Has soothed old Lehi's raging, flaming mind,
And brought him once again to sanity,
That we might now return to Jacob's Land...."
    "And to our pleasures in Jerusalem?
Which in our absence lie in dust?" the other
Sly rejoined in whispered tones that reached
Not Sam's awaiting, guileless ears. "Why not?
'Twere just as well that we enjoy the wealth
And luxuries of wealth there cumulate."
    Again young Sam enjoined: "Laman, must
You always so in bitter humor jest
About our father's dreams and words and acts?
Have they not proven prophetic, true?
Have they not led him justly through his life?
Why should you doubt their efficacy now,

Merely because they draw you from a life
Of greed? Perhaps some greater treasures lie
Before us in the Land to which we steer;
Undoubtedly before us hardships lie,
Hardships sore and sorrows plentiful;
Why not expect then joys commensurate,
Perhaps great joys and happiness? Should we
Not trust his word who first amassed our gold,
Who rightfully *his* back upon it turned,
That what he does to our eternal joy
And benefit must surely now conduce?"

"Another Nephi!" Laman barked, his voice
Hoarse with bitter humors. "Lemuel, behold!
Another Nephi! to preach to us this day
Of Heaven's revelations to the mind
Of one who in his sleep would thus be deemed
A Prophet of the Plains, a Sage of Sands,
A Desert-homed Divine, A Prince of Tents."

To whom Sam in righteous anger spake,
Denouncing deep injustices within
Wry Laman's voice: "Speak not against him so,
Bold Nephi, youngest brother of us four
Who share great Lehi's Name; for he it is
Who bears that name most proudly, with great hopes
Of high achievements through unmeasured strengths
(Strength in his arm of flesh and in his God),
That Fame redoubled, trebled it if be,
Devolve upon our father's hoary head
To bless him with undying Name as one
Engravéd in the records of this folk,
To whom Posterity may sometime turn
For true ensample and enlightenment.
Our brother is but young, a boy in years
Though man in body and in might; and if
He place his credence in the powers of Dreams
By night or day, in visionary Sights
By old and wise men seen, though to the rest

Of sad mortality invisible,
If Nephi choose so to believe, what harm,
To you can e'er result? At least he lives
As if the Wilderness were his true home,
Abode secure from cruel civility
That makes of neighbors strangers, if not foes,
Because between them lies a patch of soil,
Between them lies a patch of molding dirt
Green-crowned perhaps with verdant vineyards cool,
Rich-flowing with the purple blood of vines
Both rare and to the taste of highest cost,
Which both do covet, neither can control
Except upon demise and death of him
Who should have been firm friend and life-time stay.
While you have reaped the fruits of vile discord
As if by *Até* sown within your hearts,
That youth whom you with ridicule and hate
Spurn, deride in all your words and acts—
'Tis he to whom we owe our lives, our strengths,
For he among us owns the hunter's skills
That brings this meat you eat with bloody haste,
His youth returns but generosity
And love for cruelty and spite, and were
It not for him and for his guileless trust
(And for his fine, unfailing Bow of Steel),
Our larders would be bare of flesh, which you,
I oft perceive, with relish eat—in spite
Of grudgedness and vocal plaints enow;
But no, contention serves no purpose now,
And we must haste unto the tent of him
Who is our guardian, mentor, and our Sire."
    Sam turned his back on Laman, Lemuel,
As if to emphasize his lack of fear,
Then spoke to them across his shoulder's arch:
"Come, brothers, let us go; for Nephi now
Is absent from our camp, atop that Mount
Which he is wont to scale as erst the Sun

With burning countenance begins his march
And headlong chariot-rush across the sky;
And yet again as gray-cloaked eventide
Her somber drapery lets fall upon
Blue Earth; and there in silent isolation
Communes with Him whose Master Hand calls forth
The Sun in pearl-pale Dawning splendor bright
To send him spinning on his way, and whose
Same Hand conceals our Earth in darkness' veil
As night begins, that weary men might rest.
'Tis not incumbent that we wait for his
Return from altared mountain-crests to us
Before we meet our father in his tent.
Come, brethren, let us cease our quarreling tones
And soon present ourselves unto our sire."
    A moment's pause, then the elder two rose
To follow Sam. And as the three returned
On paths well-worn beneath tall, gleaming palms
To face great Lehi, man of suffering,
Man of sorrow, now nomadic in
Parched wastes, behold, Aurora's rosy glow
Slow-died into stark, leaden hues of Day;
And from the mountain's height young Nephi came,
With beardless, tan-browed visage deep in thought
Concerning that revealed in Morning's still
To him on sacred heights before his Lord.
Unerringly the youth, with native grace
And godly dignity, approachéd nigh
The tent of him who led them from the land
Of David's Throne, of great Jerusalem—
Lehi's tents, for in these visions seen
By Nephi on the Mount, through solemn prayer,
Before that altar to the Living God
Of Israel upraised, it was made known
Unto the mighty youth that some stern task
Was yet to come to him while dwelt the men
In Lehi's band within green vales near Moses'

Sea confined; with filial piety
The son drew near, and when he had approached
His father's place, the father welcomed with
Excess of love and confidential voice.
    Within the tent, brown-tinted sunlight's glow
Lay warm, already warm and warning of
Day's heat, reflecting on the stolid face
Of Lehi and the anxious forms of youths
Now opposite, three youths still child-like seeming
Next the gray-beard lines of Lehi's face, and
The youngest of the four sat near his side.
Lehi watched in silence; at a signal
Known only to himself, he nodded. Laman,
Lemuel, and Sam stood up as one, with
One smooth, fluid motion, and departed;
Lehi sat alone with Nephi bold; and to
His youngest son, with murmured, solemn words
(And he alone heard Lehi's whispered words)
The Patriarch thus spake: "Nephi, son,
My heart rejoices in your strength, which testifies
Of Heav'n's favor and grace from Him bestowed
From Whom all goodness flows, as flowed sweet milk
And honey spoken of by faithful spies,
Joshua and *Caleb* strong, who braved
Dark dangers in the Promised Land to bring
To their Prophet proof of Earth's fecundity,
Who after forty days in Hebron's Land,
Among gigantic sons of *Anak*'s loins,
Returned to Moses on flat Paran's Plain
(Where Israel's encampment lay) and spake
Against the fears of *Shammua*, the words
Of *Shaphat, Igal, Palti, Gaddiel,*
Of *Sethur, Anmiel,* and *Geuel,*
Who with *Nahbi*, with weak *Gaddi* stood
To counsel Israel against attempts
To wrest the Promised Land from *Anak*'s grasp,
From Jebusites, Amalikites, and men

Called Amorites, who in high mountains dwelt;
Yea, such were Spies who counseled servile fear
Until great Caleb, *Jephurneh*'s son, spoke out
At Joshua's side; and Israel's God appeared
To Sinai's Shepherd, blessing those whose faith
And true report had urged frail, erring Sons
Of Abraham to seek their Heritage,
To gain the Promised Land; and thus it was
That of great Hosts whom Mizraim fled in haste
But two survived harsh wanderings to see
And touch the Home of Israel's ancestry;
Joshua and *Caleb* true survived
And entered into their Inheritance.
   "Now we travel to another land,
Far from precious soils which were our home
And shall be but rich booty to the might
Of predatory beasts foretold
By *Jeremiah* and myself, and others
Who received fell Visions from our Lord;
We travel in the Promises of God,
Revealed to me as Patriarch within
The Eternal Order of the Universe,
Toward a second Promised Land, where we,
Where e'er it be, shall prosper and become
A mighty fold before our Lord, while they—
The Jews who crouch in David's Capital,
Beneath gray shadows of that edifice
Erected by wise, peaceful scion of
God's warlike King, he who first defiled
Pure lands with idols formed of heathen gods,
Procuréd through his wives, erected on
The summit of *Adonai*'s Eminence—
While they must dwindle in captivity,
We shall grow a mighty People, whose Seed
Shall prosper throughout time, to bring to pass
Great miracles, high wonders in the days
When He who is the Lamb shall come to Earth,

Messiah long foretold, Anointed *Christ*;
And yet I fear that this shall never be,
Unless one thing, one consequential thing
Now missing is supplied; and for this task
Your elder brothers, Laman, Lemuel,
And Sam (though he less obstinate than they
And willingly would go, though not in face
Of their recalcitrance, their wills opposed
To his desires, to mine, and to our God's)
Are doubtful, fearful of life's consequence
And of grave peril to themselves thereby.

    "Behold, my son and my delight! a Dream
Has visited me by night, in which my Lord
Has spoken and commanded me that I,
Or those by me ordained, return again
To gray Jerusalem; and I desire
That Laman, Lemuel, Sam, and you shall go,
And there accomplish that for which this Dream
Was sent. Know now, within strong, stony walls
There dwells our kinsman, *Laban*, he who with
The other Elders of the city rules
And counsels *Zedekiah* King; and they
Were they who dared suggest alliance base
With southern pagans of far-flooding Nile,
The broken Reed of Memphian suzerainty,
With *Egypt*, once our masters, now our pit
In which we lie entrapped, the straw and mud
With which the North shall augment her Empire,
As she with lightning force shall sweep across
Judæan plains, throw down our fortress walls
As if they were of sun-baked dirt, not stone,
And face to face accost the ancient might
Of him who wears the Double Crown of North
And South. This Laban is a wealthy man;
Within his house lie precious things not wrought
By Israel's craftsmen's hands but bought with gold
From lands far hence, exotic lands which few

Might name and fewer yet have seen; yet in
His house lies nearly unobserved the greatest
Treasure, that which now I seek to have,
Must have, if we are to survive the years
As faithful souls and children of our God.
That of which I speak I did not know
Was kept—although I had heard whisperings
Of it—until I saw it in a Dream
And heard the Voice of Him explain our need
To carry it with us. Into Brass Plates,
Smooth Plates of rich-worked and gold-seeming Brass,
Has Laban cut the record of our Line,
Who we are, and from whence sprung, and this he
Did long years ago, when once he, too, heard,
Understood, acceded to our Father's
Highest Will; these Plates of Brass, this record
Must be brought and with us cherished as
We wend our way into the Wilderness.
    "And now, behold, your brethren heard my words,
And scoffed, and said it was too hard a thing for them,
This thing which I desire, that they return
And bring bright plates which Laban hordes; for they
Do not perceive that I alone require
Not this thing, but God; and you, my son,
Who murmur not against the Lord, His Hand
Shall guide you in this task, that you not fail."
    As Nephi heard the words which Lehi spoke,
He lowly bowed before his aging sire
In just humility, and uttered words
Which soothed the aching sorrow left behind
By elder sons' refusal to accept
Deity's Desires in human spheres;
With fervent heart the beardless youth replied:
"My father, I will go and do the things
Which God commands of me, for I now know
That no commandment comes from Him unto
The Children of His Sons unless it be

That He prepare a way for them, that they
Fulfill the things which He demands."
    As aged Lehi heard these humble words,
His heart burst forth in joy and song unto
The Lord, in song and joy unto the Lord;
For thus he knew that Nephi's willing soul
Was open and receptive to sweet workings
Of the Spirit's power; that his Visions
Would become Reality through this Youth's
Faith and Constancy; and that his God—
The God for Whom great Lehi had left all
And dwelt in desert ways in rude-walled Tents—
Had blessed this youngest, favored male child.

BOOK III

At Dawn, Lehi bids farewell to his sons, blessing and warning them according to their obedience and their worthiness; Their preparations complete, the four sons depart on their journey to Jerusalem.

As Morning spread her ruddy Orient glow
Across low, lucent, Eastward-gleaming skies,
Across soft, pearly skies (once thought the blush
Of *Memono*'s Mother, Goddess of Pale Dawn,
As she awoke and left her rose-strewn couch,
Her couch of thornless, fragrant-scented buds
Which erst she shared with him who never died
But lived forever, ever growing old—
False immortality and wasted wrack
Of God's Eternal Plan—ever-withering
Tithonus, Prince of Troy, until at last
She left his whitened head to age's pains
And sought for fresher, younger Love while he,
Reduced to chirping husk, lived on)—at Dawn,
Bright Birth of Day, to invoke high blessings of
The Father-Seer before their backward trek,
Four sons of Lehi met before the tent
Wherein their Father wonted was to sleep;
Wonted, yes—but on this morn of hope
Dull Sleep had fled, banished with alacrity
Unto cold, dusky rest in *Morpheus'* Cave;

With leaden wings Sleep cleft Day's angled beams,
And bore his soporific charms in haste—
In haste laborious and cruelly cramped—
From realms of eager wakefulness high-pitched
Of sleep-expelling anxiousness and hope,
From hence, while Father Lehi stood before
His sons, alert and deeply sensitive
To those demands that from his God exhaled
And those upon him thrust by failing faith,
Low confidence so evident in two,
His eldest, who denied pure Pow'rs of God,
As did rash scoffers who in *Noah*'s time
Refused true evidences sent by God
Of man's degenerate and wicked state,
Who chose instead to die in horror's tears
When Heaven's Fountains wept and unrestrained
Mingled precious moistures with the Deep,
Mingled tears Celestial with Earth's
Salt Fountains of the Oceans and wide Seas;
And who in spirit-bondage fell remained
Until should come the One through whom all Pow'r
Of innocence and souls' renewal flowed,
Who in His Spirit's Pow'r and Name should strike
With blinding force through Death's long, lightless halls
And burst the Prison of Earth's buried ones;
So now, in his great age, the father stood
Before two sons who, in his prescient sight,
From one strait pathway swerved into the Dark,
And in confusion lost their Brightness high,
And in confusion lost their Birthright high
In favor of two younger, righteous sons.
    Thus stood the Desert Patriarch, his feet
Within their leathern sandals firmly riemed
And thrusting 'gainst wind-weathered stones, still cool—
Or rather, not yet heated by cruel flames
Of desert day and scorching rays of white
Which devoured unwary travelers

As *Jove*, flamed Arbiter of Sky and Light,
Appearing in the fullness of his glory
And his might, consumed that foolish maid,
Semele, condemned by *Juno*'s wiles
And jealousy, but saved her half-formed son,
Twice-born *Bacchus*, and secreted the child
Within the hollow of his thigh until
Sweet Nymphs of Nysa undertook its care
And nurturing; so also now the Sun
Reserved his lethal darts for later use
When at high mid-day he his course pursued
Along the crest of Heaven's Vault and looked
With aweful fire upon heat-wasted lands
(Lands such as rich-soiled *Lydia* named,
Which host and parent was to that fell beast,
Compound Lion-Goat, with Serpent's tail,
Whose breath unguarded withered plains until
Bellerophon, in Pegasean flight,
At *Iobates*'s call the monster slew,
Chimæra with his mighty hand destroyed—
Then in his haughty pride himself was thrown
To Earth from his pretentious seat before
The Gates of High Olympus' Mountain peak,
A Nimrod vaunting upward to become,
Through force of arms, not right, one as the Gods);
Yea, now the Sun held back his potent fires
As *Jove* his mightier thunderbolts reserved
For battles with the enemies of those
Who sojourned in immortal blissfulness
On Mount Olympus' heights, and with him took
On his most tragic mission to frail love
Pale, lesser bolts—which brilliance nonetheless
O'erwhelmed the mortal body of the Maid
Whose rosy son was fostered on wild milk
Of strangers in a hidden forest cave,
An echo of great *Abraham* himself,
Secreted by God's unallaying Will

Within a Cave from *Nimrod*'s wrath, who slew
Small Innocents to wrest his kingdom and
His life from infant hands that would one day
Defeat him in pitched battle, infant hands
That gained their strength from angels' fingertips.
Thus sheltered by the shadows of his tent,
Cave-like darkness in the desert's heat,
Great Lehi stood in morning's lucent glow,
Tenacious in his struggle to survive,
In his unyielding battle with the Wastes,
To lead his family to a land foreseen
And promised him; and thus the Prophet spake:
    "My sons, *Sariah*, wife of youth and my
Companion in old age, my daughters fair,
And you who come as servants on this trek,
Who share with me this utter Wilderness,
This isolation drear where Bitterns dwell
And screech into a thirsty, shriveled sky
Their challenge to immensities of wind,
To loneliness and to harsh, burning sands,
I speak strong words to you which I must speak,
Constrained by Him who moves and acts beyond
Dim comprehension of all humankind,
This day I send my sons, my lovéd sons,
Up to massed, sessile Jews who dwell within
The walls of Jebus, David's capitol;
To *Laban*, that they might obtain Brass Plates
Which bear the lineage of our fathers' rights,
Which shall inform us of our lawful place
Within God's House of Israel, that we
Might knowingly partake in those high vows
Which He proclaimed in truth unto our sire,
Our great Progenitor, he whose grandson
Received his name from God, and thus became
Great *Israel*—these records we must have,
For if we do not know our Heritage
We shall decline in this vast wilderness,

Failing to fulfill the destiny
And high intents reserved for us. My sons,
My Dreams have led us to this waiting Waste;
They now dictate this journey back unto
That place which sought to take my life by force
When I proclaimed near dissolution of
The Chosen Seed of Abraham and, worse,
Their fell Captivity by Northern Kings
Who worship falsely gods of graven stone
And bow to him who is dread King of Night,
Whose powers are concentrate in Northern Plains.
This task is fraught with peril, that you know
And understand. And now, before you leave
To make your way across worn paths of Death,
I would that you should heed my words, for they
Shall be a source of strength and comfort if
You share their wisdom—a stone of stumbling if
You choose to trust in human thought instead."
    Here agéd Lehi turned to face two sons,
The pair which came as blessings to his youth
When he and mild *Sariah* beauteous
First felt the stir of passion's tender fires
And acted as befit their wedded bond;
Yet now these sons afflicted Lehi's soul,
For he perceived their bitterness, their hate
And fear of righteousness and good; thus spake
Aged Lehi manfully, persuasively,
That Laman and sly Lemuel might yet
Repent, and share Salvation's Ecstasies:
"To you, my eldest, *Laman*, *Lemuel*,
I first address my heart and mind. I fear
For you, my Visions troubled and my Dreams
Obscured. Remember, o my Sons, the words
I spoke as first we found this fertile vale
Amongst wild desolation and dread thirst,
As first we saw bright, sparkling life within
Swift-flowing streamlets mingle with the Seas;

Remember, o my Sons, my Fountain-Song,
The *Quisdah* that I sang when first we stood
Together here: '*Laman, o that thou might be
Like unto this river pure, forever
Flowing from the Fount of Righteousness;
And Lemuel, o that thou too might be
Like unto this valley, steadfast, firm
In keeping all Commandments of our God.'*
I spake those words of hope and warning strong
In fear, for you have murmured oft against
Our Lord; and now I see great hardships and
Defeats unless you in humility
Yourselves deliver to His guiding Hands.
Listen and remember, o my Sons; heed
Sure promptings of that Spirit which shall come,
Shall flow upon your heads as water from
True, living streams into salt seas, for thus
And thus alone may you partake in life,
And taste sweet fruits of Truth eternally."
    Thus Lehi in full righteousness and love—
Righteousness of man and love parental—
High expressed toward two wayward scions
Of his line, toward those sons whose lives
Gave evidence of misplaced faith,
Faith in man and his accomplishments
Instead of in the steely arm of God;
And they to whom he spake stood silent by,
With muted plaints and low'ring visages,
Envenomed with flushed poisonous flames of shame
As wrathful blush envermeiled swarthy cheeks;
For more than once had they been so accused
Of less than faithfulness in serving God;
Now shame and angry fear contended in
The brethren twain for high supremacy—
And hardened hearts encased within their breasts
Of stone excluded with conspicuous force
Just shame, 'til only anger's blast remained

To flare with raging heat in future years
(With resultant murder, rapine base)
Against their father's sons to whom clear words
From God's great Prophets' tongues brought shame
And guilt, that shame which ends not in sham sorrow
Of the world, but Sorrow in the Lord,
And leads to virtue and to righteousness,
Through Faith's redemptive powers and cleansing force,
By true Repentance manifest in lives.
    And now the aged father turned to him,
The third, companion to the fourth in faith,
Sam, whose love and trust were lent in kind
To Nephi and to Nephi's innocence;
To whom the father thus: "My son, my joy!
You little speak, and never in complaint
Against high-formulated laws of Him
Who reigns Omnipotent. In all you show
Your faithfulness, your love toward Him who
All love and faithfulness deserves, and who
With merit high and guidance absolute
Shall lead you safely through dim paths ahead
Which clouded and confused in darkness lie,
By mists of deep futurity obscured,
Across Time's silent, arid wilderness,
And point to promised joys and great delight.
My son, my heart rejoices for your sake,
For in my Dreams by night which come to me,
And in those Visions resting in my eyes
Despite the piercing glare of sunlit day,
Behold, in all do you in honor pure
And youthful virtue strong appear; and yet
I would that you more steadfast stood in truth,
Less swayed by words persuasive, error-bound,
Forth-spewed by elder tongues; yea, thus my son
Should you to righteousness adhere, that thus
Might He bear witness to a father's soul,
A soul with love and anxiousness endowed

Toward those spirits given me by Him,
Great Father of men all, that you, my son,
Do tread that strait, sure path of righteousness.
Endure, my son, and persevere in Truth."
   Sam, listening intently, eyes firm-fixed
Upon his father's eyes of glowing coal,
Felt pride, and little guilt, and anger none
At all, for well he knew his father's love,
Love tempered with firm justice, and he knew
That all by Lehi spoken was the truth,
And he remembered moments lost, when he
Had failed to stand and speak for righteousness—
No vicious acts performed, nor cowardice
Displayed, but simply stood and did not act,
Chose not to work toward a greater good.
He dropped his gaze in sign submissive that
Great Lehi's words were warning, blessing both,
And in his heart mild Sam decreed that he
Would follow righteousness, would seek out ways
To support the strength of Lehi's dreams.
This Lehi saw and knew, and murmured one
More final word of love and praise for Sam.
   With that the Prophet turned his agéd eyes—
Eyes still sharp and clear, within whose glaze
No mists of watery rheum beclouding flowed
To sever mental powers from wider realms
Of Sight and Vision's majesty; just so
The Shepherd-Prophet, he who with his staff
And outstretched arm above wild water's brow
Pointed at the Eastern Wind, *Eurus* named,
And brother of all winds—rude *Borea*,
Whose dusky wings upheld his ravished bride
'Til *Orithyia* wed her ice-flamed King
In Northern climes severe; *Flora*'s lover,
Zephyrus, the West, slayer of that youth
Beloved of *Phœbus*, purple *Hyacinth*,
At whose sad death a blood-stained Flower appeared

In sorrow eloquent for blasted life;
And *Notus,* of the South, of whom are hissed
Through all high realms of Middle-Earth and Sky
But secret whisperings; these, the winds,
Bestowed with life and power by ancient myth,
Participated with Earth's mortal kind
And, through their breathed intrusions in this Sphere,
Forever altered latent History
To bring about the true Reality;
Yet none so true as Israel's history,
As twice in Moses' hegiratic flight
From Mizraim's teeming, flooded river-plain
Him winds supported, blowing o'er the wastes
Lost migratory flocks of fleshy quail,
Or furrowing a path across the sea,
Furrowing across its wrinkled face
A way to safety and escape from foes—
Yea, then as Moses reared his sovereign staff,
The Eastern Wind, by sentient force propelled,
Played upon the Sea, made wet Seas dry land,
And wat'ry elements with force disjoined;
He it was whose solid tread and sure
Vast flocks of captive Israel between
Two glassy walls compelled; he it was
Who wandered forty years in desert lands
For Israel's redemption from cruel bonds
Of pagan *Ra*; up he strode, from plains
Outstretched of Moab, with the son of Nun,
Joshua, unto that Mount called *Nebo*,
To the top of Pisgah, towering o'er
Old Jericho and guarding rich-soiled lands
To Dan bequeathed, and Naphthali; high o'er
Those portions set aside for Joseph's sons,
And o'er far lands of him through whose pure line
The Savior of the World His form of flesh
Would gain; from heights of Nebo's summit smooth,
From Abirim, beyond cool Jordan's play,

He peered with heart prophetic and clear eyes,
Across heat-wasted, treeless barrenness
On salt-stained, dying shored, across the muddy,
Turgid Jordan's flow, across age-wrinkled,
Blasted hills, to view with anxious hope
White-towered Bethlehem, where Angels' songs
Should one day rend soft, stilly night-time skies
with praising hymns, *Hosannas* to the King
In humble manger born to Maiden sweet;
And further yet the Prophet-Guide could see,
Beyond low walls which Him encompass should
Unto the far horizon's misty blue,
The far horizon's indistinctness blue,
Unto the plain where earth and sky seemed merged
And where appeared—as if a splendid dream
In marble-brightness clothed—high white-washed walls,
The mud-brick city of cruel Jebusites,
Jebus named, and *Salem* called, the *Place*
Of Peace, whereto the *Prince of Peace* should come,
A city built upon the sacred Mount
Soon *Zion* named, and later temple-crowned,
Destined at all Time's Meridian
To crucify its God, the Son of Man.
These Moses saw as he ascended lone
Mount Pisgah's highest eminence, with weight
Of heavy years upon his bowéd back,
Yet was his eye not dimmed, nor was his force
Grown less, that he should pass through Death unto
That unknown land from whence but few return
To warn mankind of future state and form,
Few, that is, until the One who burst
The veil affixéd firm between two worlds,
Who reinspired with Godly breath dead dust
Which lay consigned to Death's dark, cold embrace
Three days; yea, Moses' eye was clear and deep,
That he might see true visions of his day
And truer Vision yet to come to pass;

Not so the great Progenitor of Truth,
Israel, who wrestled with Earth's Lord,
For he in his old age would lay his hand
Upon bowed heads of Joseph's sons to bless
Them as the Lord directed, but could not
Distinguish one from other, for the eyes
Of Israel were dim for age, so that
He could not see; yet notwithstanding this,
His trembling hands unerringly progressed
And crossed, and *Ephraim*'s head received the touch
That gave to him the birthright of the line
Of *Israel* (blessings forfeited
By Reuben), and the Name of *Abraham*,
Of *Isaac*, and of *Israel's God*; even so
Stood Lehi now before his sons to bless
And Pray, and in his heart he savored long
Deep Visions of his youngest son, sure hopes
And promises of greatness in sweet lands
To which their Lord should lead them and in which
Young Nephi should become a Priest-Judge to
A mighty and delightsome Folk until
In time, and in the fullness of old age,
He should unto his God return, receive
Full glories of his righteousness. To him
Thus Lehi spake, his hands untrembling on
Bold Nephi's head: "My son, my youngest son,
To you my words are few, for you have shared
True Witness of my Visions' strength and sight.
Much you know, for you have seen; unto you
Our God has condescended to reveal
His high and sovereign Will. Much you now know,
And yet not all; before you lie long years
Of joy and sorrow, hope and fear, of love,
Of life, of death; and in those years, my son,
Shall you behold the glories of this earth,
Of vast Eternity, and of our God,
Which is Eternity, and Life, and All.

THE NEPHIAD, BY MICHAEL R. COLLINGS * 49

Nephi, open now your heard and mind;
Be guided by my words. You are favored
Highly of the Lord—live up to this high
Heritage in all you do; listen well
And with swift promptitude obey in *all*
Which may to you in form of Law Divine
Appear. Remember always, you do not
Yet comprehend in their totality
The unceasing plans of ruling Heav'n for men;
Be strong and treasure all the Laws of God.
Obey, and hidden secrets shall be yours,
Revealéd by *Adonai*'s holy mouth,
Revealéd by the Presence of the Lord."
    With final breath of benediction low,
Lehi stopped and stretched his arms out wide
To bid his sons—to bid his four loved sons—
Farewell, his father's heart compressed in sorrow
For sore trials yet before them strewn;
And in his heart he pondered dangerous paths
Before them flowing to unknown success
Beyond the mortal knowledge of his sight;
As King *Ægeus* pondered when his son,
Bold slayer of the Cretan Minotaur,
Theseus, Ariadne's lover and
Betrayer, with seven of the choicest sons
And seven virgins pure and beauteous—
Greatest treasure of the Athenian state—
As human-tribute to cruel Minos, King
Of Crete, with sails of sable hue set forth
To save his people from the Monster's maw,
The wrath and hunger of the *Minotaur*,
To whom Greek youths and maids should serve as feast.
In fear *Ægeus* saw his son depart,
Set watch upon wild, wine dark seas that bore
Him hence, in anguish threw himself into
That Sea as sheets of mortal black appeared,
The signal prearranged that his true son

Had died within high Labyrinthine walls—
Signals false, for Theseus lived; but death
Held not his heavy, leaden hand, and struck
The sorrowful King with maddening despair.
    Thus stood the Prophet-Patriarch as four
Completed preparations to depart;
His benison given, Lehi sought his tent,
The close-aired solitude afforded by
Thick walls of skins, to ponder and to pray,
To think upon his family of sons
Soon to face harsh rigors of a trek
And swift return to high Jerusalem
And massy walls o'erlooking Kidron's flow;
For Lehi, through the prescience of his Dreams
And Knowledge granted through smooth Visions' fires,
Assuréd was of full success, though at
What cost in wealth or lives to him unclear;
Wide vistas of futurity lay still,
Deep beclouded by altérnate paths
Before his sons displayed—their own free will
And high-bestowed Agency must guide
Them as a cord through Labyrinthine dark
And back again into gray desert wastes;
From *David*'s Jebusitic citadel,
So soon to fall beneath Oppressors' force,
Unto the freedom-giving solitude
Of blesséd Judah's buffer-wilderness.
In the darkness of the tent, unseen by
Mortal eyes—though witnessed by high Hosts
Of Intelligences, Spirits waiting
To be clothed in flesh, eager to be clothed
In fragile flesh and to partake the joys
And pains of this Mortality in spite
Of all the suffering it entails, eager
To pursue the next full step in their
Eternal portion of the Plan, yet knowing

In their hearts great Lehi's grief—the Angels
Watched as he wept tears of sorrow for his sons.

BOOK IV

The sons attain their Father's home near the walls of Jerusalem without incident; The elder two would enjoy the luxuries they find, but Nephi reminds them of their task and urges diligence in completing it; Laman angrily silences his brother and claims the honor of obtaining the Plates for himself; As Lemuel, Sam, and Nephi wait outside the city walls, Laman enters Jerusalem to speak with Laban.

DESCEND from Heav'n, *Urania*, from Spheres
Beyond all ken of brief Mortality;
Descend to me, uplift, and bear away
With flight Celestial my willing soul
Beyond all cares that bind men to dense Earth,
Beyond these salt-stained reaches of the Sea
That now the sons of Lehi would desert;
Bear me with swifter pace than Camel's sway
To peopled Realms and walls of mortised stone
Surrounding smooth-paved Temple courts, dim streets,
And noisome, pestilential multitudes;
Nor suffer my high thoughts to fail, that I—
Deprived of Wisdom and of patience's Sight,
As one forlorn and lone, Aleian fields
Need never stray—and me defend from flights
Too near the jealous majesty of gods,
Of *Zeus* who rash *Bellerophon* condemned
To blindness' fears, of *Athene* Angered
Who transformed *Arachnid* charms to leggy
Horror for attempting to compete

With high Olympian skills; let me not aim
Too near their unexpressive light, too near
Their Light and fall as *Phæton* Helios-born,
Who ventured to command swift Sun-steeds' flight
Against the wiser council of the gods;
Or *Icarus,* that heedless child of wise,
Sciential *Dædalus* who egress found
From Minos' Labyrinth but fell through his
Own elemental pride and tumbled on
Soft-waxen wings unto his doom; but on
Thy tireless wings, thy wings substantial,
Yea, wafted on thy ceaseless, in-breathed Pow'rs
Remain, ne'er needing bridle magical
To rein thee, spur thee on to greater Heights
Beyond the springing Well of Helicon;
Yea, come, Celestial One, that I above,
From a stony altar crowning Nephi's
Place of meditation's sanctity,
On crested heights above the encrusted marge
Of waves by *Moses*' Power compelled to part
And pass dry-shod great hosts of Israel;
From this high altar's base my watchful eye
Cast o'er the thirsty sparseness of sere plains
And timid verdure of that stream-fed vale
Which hosted the nomadic Prophet's tents—
From such inspired heights as I might reach
Upon the pinions of my Muse Divine,
My eye would pause in conscious, stirring thought
As four well-laden beasts of burden moved
With stately march, led all by men mature
(Save one, whose guide, though large and powerful,
Was youthful nonetheless), from Lehi's tents
Into far, golden reaches of the Waste
Where distant mounds of swelling stone-girt hills,
Blue-shimmering beneath the searing eye
And withering heat of the Arabian sun,
Merged, melted with deluding hue

Into deep-toned cerulean that stained
The vaulted sky-dome's high immensity,
Into this void the sons of Lehi strode,
Retracing steps achievéd first through toil
And thirsty suffering, just as in
That Tartarean, pagan underworld,
Hades, dread and black abode of him
Who with his fellows—brother-gods supreme—
Shared sovereignty o'er all created Earth;
In that Hell of dark antiquity,
Sisyphus performed his weary task,
Rolling his huge stone up to the crest
Of Hades' Hill, to have it by some force
Unseen, unfelt by any shade but he
Repulsed and thrust headlong again into
The Stygian depths where he must now descend,
Begin anew his levied punishment,
Ne'er resting, save but once, when all of Hell
Gained respire from tormenting, deathless pains
As sweetened tones of love from *Orpheus*' lyre
Invaded all deep, mournful, silent depths,
Touched dull and long-unfeeling hearts of shades
And filled their emptiness with memories
Of Love; for sweet *Eurydice* was dead
And *Orpheus* through Cerberean Gates
Had pressed, to plead with *Pluto*'s sorrowing Queen,
Had made his Harrowing way through crowds of shades
Awaiting each with hopeless heart a breath
 Of living air from Earthly glades to cheer,
To comfort fast-imprisoned ones; on through
Thick darkness passed the living Man, to depths
Where Light of Sun ne'er rent the Veil of Night,
Where he who ruled with force the Realms of Death
Upon his iron throne awaited One
Who came to ravage Death's Domains and bear
Again to life a captive soul; to her
He turned, *Proserpine*, black Queen,

And tuned his lyre to more than mortal song;
'Til *Orpheus*' sweet harmonies devised
That deeply bored into unfeeling hearts,
Drew iron tears from Death's unweeping heart,
And made Hell grant what *Love* had *Voice* to sing—
And who with Lycidean grace was raised,
Lifted to become an adumbration
Of the *Christ*, true *Genius* of the Shore.

    Thus as the ancient *Sisyphus*, whose toil
In Hades oft repeated was, the sons
Of Lehi turned their steps again toward
Their home, Jerusalem. With tents and stores
Sufficient for their desert trek they strode—
For these were no unlawful, raiding ones
Who lightly traveled, without cumbrous tents,
To ravage and to steal with lightning force
As would wild, fierce, nomadic Western tribes
(The fallen sons of sons of *Laman*'s sons,
To whom in Latter-days would surely come
The Voice of one who spake from Ages past,
The Voice of one who speaks as from Earth's dust
And brings to their remembrance Covenants
Between their Fathers and the Lord of Hosts,
Until in their enlightenment again
The savage Lamanites become a folk
Of pleasure—pure, delightsome, light
In Spirit, light in Soul, in Heart); or
Asiatic hordes who flooded Eastern steppes
Beneath the staring eyes of Golden *Khan*s,
Of Potentates who all destroyed to gain
What they but little valued after death,
And swept without restraint into the West
To pillage and destroy Civility;
Or *Northmen* savage who from Geatland
And Jutland sailed in hawk-swift wooden ships
Across the *Whale-Road* to plunder coasts
In search of dragon-hoards, of red-blood gold,

Of arm-bands glorious, and shields strong
To bear their name and fame beyond this life;
Not so the sons of Lehi, merchant-sons,
Who took with them their tents into waste wilds,
Who moved with conscious speed but not that haste
Of men cast out from Man's society,
Of men through ostracism's ban cast out,
Denied by fatal sign on shells incarved
The comfort and security of tribe,
Forced rather to rely on self, on powers
Inherent in their frames to stave off death
Pursuing closely on their swift-flung heels
As angered yeomanry its just revenge
For acts asocial, dangerous should seek—
Not so the sons of Lehi moved, but sure
And carefully, yet without hesitation,
With necessary speed they crossed the land,
The parching land, murderous and cruel,
Halting as the desert harsh decreed,
Up to the margent soil of Judah's kings,
Up to the towers of David's fortress-walls,
Up to the seat of *Zedekiah* King
And streets that Laban's treasure-house contained.
    And yet they passed not through the city's gates,
For Lehi dwelt not so among the Jews;
Across smooth Kidron from the Templed Mount,
There dwelt the Prophet-Patriarch in peace,
Still near enough to Holy Heights to join
His fellow merchants in their daily trade,
But in an exile self-imposed from massed
And crowded, pressing streets within stone walls,
Where evening breaths might unobstructed flow
Among thick gray-green leaves of olive trees,
Upon white balconies and upper rooms
With hints of coolness after savage heats.
Thus as slow, softening palls of night-time gray
Descended o'er red-flaming, opal skies,

Lehi's sons saw again their fathers' home,
Met again dear servants left behind
To care for lands and beasts until such time
As others would assume complete control
Of Lehi's garnered wealth. And as the flocks
At eventide sure safety of the fold
And shepherd's patient, loving care enjoy,
And swiftly turn before feared night descends
With threat of predator and hungry death
From lion's claws or ragged fang of wolf,
So entered with the dying sun the four
Within their walls' protective strength and power
To Lehi's sumptuous home, once scene of youth
And happy childhoods spent; now silent, still,
Awaiting yet loved press of master's tread.
    Within the beckoning walls two strode in haste,
Dusty, caked with heat and desert sand,
Eager for lush luxuries of wealth
Long left behind and long looked forward to;
Laman and his brother Lemuel,
Sybaritic pair, whose only thoughts
Were of sweet, splendid wines and linens soft,
Of rich repast and lustful feasts prepared,
Of chambers cool within their white-walled home.
Not so the younger twain, smooth-cheeked Nephi
And mild Sam, whose thoughts entire to their task,
Unto their father's Heav'n-instructed Call
Entrusted and commissioned them, were cast;
And as the bearded, coarsened elder pair
Their preparations made for carnal joys
And satisfaction of their gnawing needs,
As Laman's voice resounded through still halls
And called impatiently for wine and food,
For meat and drink and olives, dates, and grapes,
Bellowed with the inward power of one
Who felt himself accustomed to command
(Or wished to feel himself skilled to command)—

As Laman's wishes echoed through the place,
Young Nephi with full strength his outcry raised,
And to them spake: "My brethren, elder sons
Of my great father's age, whose strength he thus
Has marshaled in his hopes of high success
In this our task; my brethren, was it thus
We crossed wide, burning wastes, for this we braved
Grave torment's perils of Judæan wilds,
Again to indulge in pleasure's slothful ease
And sensual delight? Did we not come,
Our father's high commandment to fulfill?
How can we thus perform our given task
With minds bemuddled by red, grapy drink
And powers debased through heedless diffidence?
Brothers, we must counsel and decide
How best we might obtain the Plates of Brass;
For this we need full faculties and might,
Since Laban will not easily concede
To our desires, enjoined though they may be
By our long-distant, visionary Sire."
    To whom the eldest spake, dark Laman spake,
Contempt concealed but thinly in his Voice,
Anger gleaming deadly in his eye,
His countenance incarnadined with ire:
"Young precious fool! who thinks to rule with youth
The high affairs of age and wisdom's bounds;
Yet fears lax impotence in him whose vaults
Protect thin scraps of Brass so valued by
Our dotard sire. Be calm, and worry not!
Our kinsman Laban loves not servile brass,
However many words it might support;
Fine, beaten gold of sulfurous, fiery gleam,
Or argent purity beriched with jewels
And diadems of crystal blood, of fire,
Of sea-foam captured in a net of flame
Alone incite within his greed-choked heart
The unquenchable heat of base avidity.

I know him well, for in my former youth
I oft was constant inmate in his house,
And then close confident of one who long
In Death's embracing arms has coldly lain;
    "Yea, I was with the son of Laban's age
When Death enfolded him, when we as peers
Upon the desert wastes with arrows armed
Our youthful manhood sought to prove in hunt;
We sought the lion, fearful beast of prey,
Nor fearing steely claw nor slav'ring fangs—
We fought the lion, foaming beast of prey,
And we two stood with arrows nocked, bows taut
As the beast with feral roar approached;
We two as friends and compeers armed stood bold,
Confronting such a beast as none but few
Had ever seen, solid in our strength and skill;
But I alone of two unharmed returned
To cold Jerusalem, while in the wastes
Gaunt Death invited all to join his feast
And share with leonine companions
The sinews and raw flesh of my bow-friend.
    "Since that day long ago I have not seen
The inner walls of Laban's home, yet know
That in remembrance of things past and dead
Our kinsman will into my hands the plates
Deliver when I ask of him this boon.
Our father fears and faints in vain 'fore him;
For one such as myself, in whom the bonds
Of true affection deep residing lie,
Our task is but a simple one indeed.
I need but ask, and what I seek is mine!"
      Thus speaking, Laman turned again his heart
To earthly pleasures and delights of taste,
With gustatory diligence applied
His rapt attention to the laden board
By servants quick prepared, and Laman ate,
With Lemuel at his side, in chairs from

Cedared Lebanon, rich-carved with coils and
Arabesques, that swirled like vines beneath their arms.
Not so the younger twain, who viewed with fear
This lack of purposiveness in Laman's mind,
This lack of purposiveness in Laman's speech;
To which young Nephi in rebuke replied:
"Not so, my brother, Eldest Brother and
Admitted Heir to Lehi's house and wealth;
Not so, for I have heard, and fear slow years
Passed by have weakened much those bonds of love;
Our father knows, and I have seen sure signs,
Of avariciousness in Laban's eyes
Of such complexion that the Plates of Brass
(If massy and if of dimension large,
Or workmanship ornate, and thus to crave)
Will yet to him appeal, and not with ease
May we succeed in wresting them from him;
And of the second matter which you vaunt,
Your boastful love of Laban's once-live heir,
Count not too much upon the strength thereof,
For *Rumor* often speaks of Laban's grief,
Faint whisp'rings touch the common ear that you
In angered Laban's eyes and heart
Sole cause were of his only son's demise,
And that for this conceit has he enclosed
From that time forth his house and heart from you;
But more than this, I fear his ancient role
As Elder of our Tribe and Keeper of
Brass Records from the past. If we the plates
Obtain, it must be through obedience
To some unknown Command of God. I fear...."
    With wrath unsheathed swart Laman severed words
That Nephi felt to speak, and smote with force
Of years his brother's beardless, youthful cheek.
    "Silence, brat! I am eldest, and I speak!"
Then sat he once again before the feast
As if bold Nephi's words were naught but air,

Empty air that one might with despite—and
Safety—permission give to pass away.
He ate a while in silence, then he spake:
"I am convinced that I alone of all
Shall never fail in any task which I
Through strength of will and fleshly might perform.
I need not gods to guide my wits and arms;
I need but that which I within me see.
Yet to allay your fearful qualms and words
This do I now propose: that we cast lots
Among ourselves, to see who should proceed—
I, the eldest, or untried Nephi who,
For all his boastful speech yet lacks a plan
By which to seize the object of our Quest.
Shall it be so? Shall we allow the gods
To choose their Champion through the roll of Chance?
For by the Prophet is it said, that man
May cast the die, but God determines what
The bones wall show. Are you agreed thereto?"
    Then in the silence deep which followed this,
The voice of Lemuel, as yet unheard,
Surged forth with words of approbation and
Advice: "My brother Laman, I follow,
As youth should follow age; to cast the lots
Is just and proper in our present cause.
And to that end I offer you my die,
Bleached bones that never yet have failed my need."
And with those words he reached beneath his cloak
And set upon the table carven bones
That should determine God's high will and choice
In matters such as this. To him Sam spake,
To Laman and to Lemuel, whose hands
Had close upon the fateful, lawful lots:
"Remember only that one mocks our God,
As you have done, at peril of great wrath
From Him who is above and hears your jests.
God may ordain another ending to

The cast of lots than you would hope to see;
Yet shall we do as you propose, that we
May soon embark upon our given task,
And bring to Lehi word of our success."
    Thus spake the younger son with wisdom high,
And at his words the three remaining signed
To ratify agreement with his thoughts—
Nor could bold Nephi and mild Sam have known
The policy determined by the two
Opposing them, that Laman should suggest
And Lemuel concur to cast the lots,
Nor could the righteous ones suspect, through their
Undaunted innocence, collusion,
Treachery, and guile as Lemuel cast,
Laman called the consequence of chance.
    The die was cast; and yet in spite of Laman's
Faithlessness, Lemuel's guile, and bones made
False by hidden weights embedded in their
Curves and surfaces, God indeed ordained
That from this act high deeds should come, though not
Through him who vaunted manly powers;
Nor from this cast should Eastern worlds resound
With war and conquest's fire, as when the man
Who dared withstand the might of Pagan Rome
And crossed blue Rubicon despite of threats,
Stood still until the rolling of bleached bones
Upon dark, barbarous soil assured him of
Great victory against the Eagle's strength;
Nay, the Eastern Hemisphere should long remain
In ignorance of scenes resultant played
By Laman and his brethren-kin upon
Far soils promised, yet unknown, for in
The act performed by Laman's will perverse,
By Laman's weening pride first struck upon,
By Laman's sleek connivance first bethought—
The casting of the lots—were sown sure seeds
Of Laman's fall, humiliation just,

And of concurrent elevation of
The youngest son through powers divine to him
Conferred in recognition of his truth,
His purity, and righteousness; yet seemed
All otherwise, for as the lot was cast,
Three younger wills were placed by Covenant
Beneath decisions by the elder made
Who first of young Sariah's womb saw light;
For of the sons, the lot supported him
Whose pride immeasured in his mortal powers
O'erpassed humility for Godly gifts.
Thus Laman won, and in his haughtiness
Upstrode unto wide gates of fragrant woods
And entered into vast Jerusalem,
Behind him hurling high-flung words to those
Who waited in night-shadowed rocks beneath
The city's walls: "Behold, I shall not fail
To seize the Plates of ancient burnished Brass;
Your wisdom is but folly, little one,
Your fears unworthy of a Hebrew man,
A son of *Abraham*'s long-chosen House;
You, Nephi, think you may command in all
Because you are the youngest born, the son
In whom aged Lehi treasures foolish hopes,
With whom he shares vague, fond imaginings;
Yet know now, *child*, that I am Lehi's heir,
His wealth and power shall come to me when he
Has breathed his last upon this useless trek;
And then I shall return unto these gates
To take my rightful place among our tribe,
Honored for my wealth and wisdom's sake;
This Laban surely knows, and thus will he
In memory of future happenings
Aid me in soothing Lehi's vain conceits
Until sure Death might quench his madman's dreams;
Thus fear you naught, for there is naught to fear!
    "Wait for me before the gates, and see

How I and I alone—without the aid
Of that hoar deity to whom you pray
With wasted breath and doubly wasted time,
Since time ill-spent upon your bended knees
Were better wended actively engaged
In bringing that about for which you pray—
I act, and in so doing thus I shall
This task with speed and without pains complete."
     Thus Laman with deep pride inborn of years
Of wealth and elder sway o'er Lemuel, Sam,
Last-born Nephi, and fair siblings of
Maternal sex, his way unto the City
Of dead Kings with forceful stride betook;
As one who heedless flaunts divine Decree
And acts in ignorance of High commands
Devised as Heaven's God and Earth's great Lord
In council joined with first-created Souls
To set wide worlds in axis-spinning tracks
Across the universe, to spread from *Kolob*,
To the farthest ends of Time and create
Dwellings for eternal, infinite
Intelligences from before the worlds
And gods began; yea, Heaven's Highest God,
And Him Own first-begotten Spirit-Son,
The only Son begotten in the Flesh
By Elohim's descendant love upon
A gentle, waiting Maid (His righteous Love,
Not rapine rude by *Zeus* within those forms
Of Swan and Bull and Golden Shower to hide
His pretexts from his victims and his
Justly angered, vengeful, Sister-Wife); thus
He, Laman, strode full unconcerned by words
And council-message countenanced by Gods,
As in the pure Empyrean where they dwell
High-throned above the turquoise globe of Earth,
Within the glassy Globe of Kolob's Sphere,
Urim and Thummim for a Universe,

Itself a source of Revelation's Fire,
Great *Elohim*, encircled by sweet Praise
Of countless Concourses of Daughters, Sons
In Spirit fine conceived and given Life
(Intelligences clothed in spirit Flesh,
Eternal Agents clothed in flesh refined)
Communed with His Anointed, ready Heir,
Lamenting Man's obsessive willfulness,
Mourning for those Souls that chose to move,
Through exercise of conscious Agency,
Away from Light, and vile Damnation sought
(As Laman seemed in his perversity
And pride to do) through Disobedience—
Obedience severe to laws and rights
And punishments by him disposed who glooms
Plutonic Underworlds, by Ancients called
With simple elegance Dead-Ruling *Dis*—
Through *Dis*obedience willful and confirmed
To Law establishéd in Justice' Right
And vigorous Decree by *Elohim*
Endowed with Guiding powers, through disregard
Of Mercy's offerings, incarnate Love
Professed by Heaven's Son and soon to be
For all Time prov'n as *Christ* should die in pain
To expiate the greater pain of Men,
To expiate the deeper pain of Sin.
Of Courts Celestial had Laman heard,
Where claims of justice undefiled were pled
Forth-issuing from Heaven's Monarchy,
And with sweet strains of Mercy admixed were
As ere this Earth received its Spirit Shape,
Its Elemental Form, the Gods convened
Through Earth, Air, Fire, Flood—the Elements
That underlie all Form, all Substances,
Or mortal-gross or Heavenly-refined—
In Council elevate, the Cause of Man,
His destiny and hope to consecrate

In favor of true-searching Souls; of this
Had Laman in his pliant youth been taught,
But now the flinty hardness of his heart,
The hardness of his proud and manly heart,
O'ercame all wisdom and o'ercame all fears;
And thus, unthinking of his course and goal,
The son of Lehi strode into the Dark.
    Nomadic Stars crossed slowly through the sky,
Weaving brilliant paths of fire into
High Heaven's silky, distant Canopy;
And still three left behind and waiting,
Yea, still three huddled deep-sequestered 'mid
Safe, shelt'ring shadows and black-covering Night,
Awaited his return whose prideful boast
Hung trembling on the heavy-silent air
Long after he, with steadfast, ringing tread
Merged slowly into vague-formed Nothingness
Within the depths of David's Capitol.
And still three waited under covering Night.

BOOK V

The Author recounts the dignity of Epic Poetry and repeats his Invocation for Inspiration; In answer, his Visions re-open and he sees Laman hurrying in fear through the streets of Jerusalem; Together with the other three brothers he returns to Lehi's house to tell his experiences with Laban and to justify his failure to attain the Plates; Laman urges return to Lehi, but Nephi counters this suggestion with arguments drawn from Hebrew history; The Author continues Nephi's arguments into the future, comparing Lehi's plight with that of the Restored Church in its Exodus from Kirtland and Nauvoo to Salt Lake City.

'TIS evening; none stirs now but I; alone
Within the silent fastness of my room,
Surrounded by soft soundlessness of sleep,
I invoke again the unfettered Muse—
Not *Calliope*, epic muse, but sweet
Urania, celestial Patroness,
Image of a Goddess-Mother—lesser
Image of a Mother-God Eternal
Whispering sustaining truths to waiting
Ears of those for whom she bore pure
Spirit flesh, enclosing immortalities
In preparation for Estates to come;
Divine precursor of poetic flights
That bear the Earth-tied Poet's searching mind

To Crystal Worlds above more common molds,
To Worlds in which carved Shepherd's Pipes of Pan
Lie mute and still, in awe before sweet power
And voice of *Orpheus*' Lyre of Love, before
The ancient Makers' chanting Voices raised
In song to warrior's deeds heroic, high,
Beyond all powers of merely mortal men.
Here dwell the great ones sung by bards of old
Who fled low Earth to range Parnassian Slopes,
Inspired through draughts from deep Pierean springs;
(But thou, *Urania*, full know that I
Thy meaning, not thy pagan *Name*, invoke)
Me to this ultra-mundane World uplift,
With those to join who to creative heights
Ascended long ago, when time was young:
'The blind old man of Scio's rocky isle,'
Homer, son of Athens, Scio, Smyrna,
And other City-States that claimed to be
His nurturer and fatherland; he
Who first of Western minds dared peer into
High realms of gods and demi-gods, that he
Of great *Achilles*' wrath, *Odysseus*' wiles
Might rhapsodize heroic—Epic—lays;
Here too Mantuan *Maro*, *Virgil* known,
From topless heights of Ilium's flaring walls—
By fire consumed and raw Achaean thirst
For glory and revenge—viewed humankind
As he, renowned for deepest piety,
Who sacrificed his Name and Heritage
To force an Empire foreordained by gods,
Æneas, great Anchises' son, let those
Who lived beyond the Fall of matchless Troy
Through battle with armed hero's flashing sword,
With *Turnus*, champion of proud Latium,
Unto a new and greater land and home,
Unto a city soon bedecked to be
In lavish hangings of the Imperial hue

Erst donned by grave *Octavian*'s forebear;
Yea, come *Urania*, Heav'nly Muse, to me,
As once to him who sightless, agéd, sat
And sang of deeds above heroic held,
Who spurned the martial deeds of epic hosts
To sing of Man and of Man's primal Fall,
By *Satan*'s guiles engulfed and blinded once,
By *Christ*'s redemptive love upraised until,
In later worlds, co-heirs with God's divine
Creative powers, made one with Christ as Christ
Is one with God—no mystic Trinity
(Unknowable, unutterable, lost
In men's contrived illogic and despair),
But one in Purpose, Scope, and Power; and Sons
And Daughters of our First Parents' joining
Raised to Thrones Celestial as witnessed
Heirs to God's own Immortality.
With Worlds to create and people through
The endless march of Time. O, come! thou Muse;
I sit and wait within the feeble Light
Of waxen-candle's flame, encircled by
Deep quiet and the listening calm of night.
    But hold! art thou so soon appeared? I see
No phantom shapes to signify thy form,
No whispered movements near soft Drapery
Dividing me from soporific Night,
No Light increasing to my sight as shafts
Of purest Light congeal within my room
As once to Joseph wise Moroni came,
More times than once, and him instructed in
Long-dissipated Nephite history,
Gave him promise of the Restoration
Of all things through him and through his faith;
Nay, none of these, and yet I surely know
My Muse has given heed and swiftly flown,
For through my midnight Pen a Spirit speaks,
And I again behold the heroic past

As fleet through narrow, shadowed city streets
A figure lone with frantic footfall runs,
Wheels along rough stony ways as one
By mortal fear and danger threatenéd;
His peering eyes, more staring back than fore,
Glow whitely in his darkened, fearful face;
His straining ears tuned to pursuing sounds
Lest unseen enemies surprise his rout,
His wild retreat from Laban's treasure house.
Up to his brothers' covert shade—and past—
Rash Laman ran, propelled by unnamed Dread,
Blinded to the path, the truth, the way.
  From deep within warm shadows surged a Voice,
A Voice as if from Darkness' vast Abyss,
Unembodied floating through Night's breath
To touch and startle Laman's straining ear;
Perceived by Laman wrongly as a sound
Endowed by Powers of black *Apollyon*,
The voice of Nephi rose to question one
Who, forth-propelled by fears of Darkness' Dread,
Thus sought escape: "My brother, stay! Return
To us and give us your report. What has
Occurred that you in fear should flee, as if
The very hosts of Satan's pit behind
With ne'er-embodied armies you pursued?"
  To whom spake Laman, pride and voice subdued,
Though anger throbbed within his timbrous tone,
And pulsing blood with racing breath conspired
To coarsen, make more harsh the whispered words:
"Not far do you exaggerate grave fear
That gripped my soul and mind; for I in truth
Have faced the hatred and dark malice fell
Of hellish wiles this night; yet will I not
In this unweaponed spot long tarry now
To speak more fully of my case; let us
Return within the shelt'ring ring of Home,
To Lehi's vacant Home, where light and food

And drink will soon restore unto my limbs
Their wonted power and might—I labor now
To further speak. Let us depart at once
And wordlessly proceed to friendlier halls."
    In fear and deep astonishment, four shapes
With ceaseless care and silent step retraced
Their paths toward ancestral lands, until
As ghost-white planes, those walls appeared that formed
The outer bulwark of great Lehi's own.
The eldest son passed speechless through broad gates,
Through doors, to disappear into dark rooms
That soon resplendently reflected light
Of oil lamps, with food and drink brought out
From Lehi's vast and rich-appointed stores.
With shaking hand and visage pale, Laman
Worried blood-red wines and honey-cakes,
Eating yet not tasting, drinking without
Savor, fear retreating slowly from
His unmanned heart. At last he spake unto
The others sitting near, words hurling sharp
And low: "Behold, as fell the causal lot to me,
I went to Laban's house within the walls,
Along those streets that often I had trod
As I, in heedless youth, with Laban's son
Great deed conceived that we as men should do;
His doors were yet unfastened against night's dark
And easily did I approach unto
The Chamber of his Presence, there to wait
Amid rich-gilded ornaments and woods
Deep-carven, fragrant with exotic scents;
And yet methought that Laban's treasured stores
Less sumptuous and fine than Lehi's wealth
Appeared, his hangings coarser, gold less pure.
Into his chamber richly robed he came,
With broidered vestments, Tyrian purple died,
His bulky grossness dignified by waves
Of precious, liquid, flowing silky garb;

Honored Laban, Elder of the Tribe,
Keeper of the Brazen Plates of Lore
And Family-Lines. Long years had lightly touched
His massive frame since last I spoke with him;
Wordlessly he stood before me, angered,
Glowering at this intrusion bold
Into his evening's sanctuary-still.
Undaunted strode I up to him, demanded
All that Lehi's visionary mind
Required; with voice and mien imperious—
Before which onslaught Laban ashen paled
And shrank affrighted beneath my piercing gaze—
I forced my will upon his eld, until
So near dear culmination of my goal,
So near accomplishment of my pursuit,
He raised a sound of anger and of fear
And summoned to his person servitors,
Who, hearing me a *Thief* and *Murderer*
Decried (for truly did you fear that he
In great injustice and deceit me for
The untimely passing of his heir and son
Accountable would hold, for reasons that
In honesty and truth I cannot form
Nor understand): yet nonetheless he cried
Me "Murderer" to his open door and to
The sleepless world without his door; yea, thus
He summoned those who with thick staves of wood
Fire-hardened and strong me from his sight
Expelled with threats of force and deadly pain;
Through David's city's streets as one accurst
I fled, until at last with mindless motion passed
I buttressed walls and breathed free desert winds;
For then, as on command, the servants paused,
Laban's fatal-minded servants paused,
Returned within the city's depths, and I,
With rushing pulse and breath progressed unto
Our meeting-place. And so it is, I say,

That we shall never now these Plates attain,
Since Laban in his hatred grows severe,
Implacable to our desires, and warned
Of our high hopes he never will consent
That they—the Plates of Brass—shall come within
Our grasp. I counsel now that we return
Unto our Father's tents and with smooth words
Persuade him of fond, foolish paths he sees
Deep-clouded in his misty Vision's scope;
He cannot longer hope to sojourn in
Thirsty wastes if we, the four of whom
He is most proud, in single mind oppose
His senile wish and him compel again
Toward these homely walls and high-beamed rooms.
Thus counsel I, the eldest, and the one
Who of us four alone the ire of Laban
Felt and knows—return without delay."
    Wordlessly the second son assented,
At a cunning glance from Laban's eyes
Lemuel assented to his base plan,
To retreat and low submission shown
The power and force of Laban's servitors
And contrivance against great Lehi's will;
For Lemuel in all submitted to
O'erbearing will and strength of Laman's words
And had since youth his Elder brother held
In high respect, servile obedience
Fearful of his brother's angered arm and
Of his brother's oft-blooded, heated blade;
But Nephi spake in opposition firm,
With marching heart and high faith forthright proven
Undaunted by his brothers' ire or age
Beneath the darkened storm-front of his brow
O'ercast with blackened thunderings of fear,
Young Nephi as a sunlit Eminence
Gleamed bright against the background of dull night,
Bright radiant courage flickering in

His deep-set, flashing eyes; and thus he spoke:
"My brother Laman, can we so forget
Injunctions of our Father's mouth that we
The Plates of Laban *must* possess, obtain;
Shall our high resolution fail because
Our kinsman has succumbed not to your will,
Has not submitted to o'erweening pride
And shared with us the Records of the Past?
Is hope then dead, and faith in God forgot
Because our first attempt has come to naught?
    "But think though Hebrew history, and man's,
To see that often deeds performed unto God's Name
Long in the offing stand before success
Is granted to the faithful, working ones.
Remember we that Shepherd-Prophet, son
(He thought) of dusky Hamite loins, scion
Of Egyptus, she who carried through
The *Deluge* darkened Blood, by Murder of
A Brother stained and weakened ever by
Pained loss of Priesthood right and Heritage;
Remember *Moses*, mighty *Amram*'s son,
Holy Priest of God through Levi's Line,
Who sucked from aging *Jochobed* his strength
Of sinew and of mind and soul; did he,
In his divine-appointed task, succeed
When first he pit his stave against black powers
Of Egypt's pagan priestly caste? Did he,
At first, show evidence of true success?
Or did he forty years in training serve
In the Courts of Memphian Kings,
Of her whose father bore the Double Crown
Supposed heir to Mizraim's rich fertility
Though son in truth to patient, suffering slaves
Who, for their friendship with the Shepherd-Kings,
Their friendship with the Hyksos' Pharaoh-King,
Incurred the Wrath of Egypt's native line
As foreign rulers from the Nile were scourged;

Yea, spent not so the man his early years
Allied with mortal enemies of Truth
Until condemned to perish in the Sands
For spilling murky blood of Egypt's own—
Yet he survived, and through his faith he lived,
Encountered kindred souls whose hearth he shared,
And with them spend his manhood's forming years,
Served forty years beneath the lowering brow
Of thunder-ridden *Sinai* as shepherd-son
To *Jethro*, high-born Priest of Midian,
Priest ordained beneath the lawful hand
Of *Caleb*, fourth removed from his who knelt
Beneath the Hand of God Himself, *Esaias*,
Who in the days of *Abraham* received
All Power to act for God from God's self-hand
And whom by *Abraham* was richly blessed
With gifts of spirit, gifts material;
And of this chain of Rights by Heaven forged
Must Moses form a vital, breathing link,
(Link vital as all living things are linked
In true progression from the Throne of God,
The Greater and the Lesser held in strictest
Measure determined by obedience,
Ascending and descending in their
Universal courses as His Wisdom
Has foreseen and ever will foresee)
Before achieving that which God decreed—
The freeing of bound sons of Israel.
Eighty years thus marched with iron tread
Before *Adonai*'s weary children-host
Could see their benefactor *Moses* awe,
With Priesthood's power, vague empty Magic forms
Resorted to by *Pharaoh*'s desperate Monks,
Devoted servants of once-Thrice-Great *Hermes*,
Himself a shadow of full knowledge gained
And shared by Father Abraham while he
Resided in Egyptian Lands, teaching

Pagan priests of Universal Circuits,
Mathematic Powers, and True Laws,
Laws by which all Worlds are governéd
Beneath the hands of Gods and Elder Gods.
   "But hold—are we to think thereby in vain
That once the mighty tide began to flow
Of people, beasts of burden, cattle, goods,
That unobstructed they obtained this Land
Of their Inheritance; with tears recall
That forty years again became dim past,
And for their sins and learned frivolities
(So dear to wandering Israel that few
With conscious Agency abandoned them
Upon Commandment of their Prophet-Priest)
The elder Generation was condemned
To die within the frightful desert Wastes;
Their sons alone, and their sons' sons, would see—
With *Miriam*'s daughters' daughters' worthy eyes—
And enter joyfully the Promised Land.
Even he, who in his white-haired age
As guide and mentor to God's Chosen served,
Who elevated at blue Heav'n's behest
The *Brazen Serpent* to redeem the flesh
Of those by fiery heat and pain consumed,
The Serpent made of *Brass* as Type of God
That brought salvation physical for those
Who would believe, just as the Plates of *Brass*
Shall Spirit-healing bring to Lehi's train
With him departed for *our* Promised Land;
Yea, even *Moses* failed to press his tread
Into the rich and fertile waiting soil
Of Israel's new homeland found; but saw
From Nebo's Heights and then translated was
Unto his God, away from mortal eyes
To live or die according to the Will
Of ruling Heav'n's and to God's Decree."
   At this dark Laman would have formed response,

Or wily Lemuel, and would have broken
Nephi's speech with cholered taunts or haughty,
High disdain; indeed, had wrenched thin lips to speak
Their fury at this upstart youngest son,
Then blanched, fell dumb, unable to continue
And thereby more inwardly infuriate
By Nephi's unassuming, just rebuke;
Nor understood the two that Angel-hands
Invisible thus stayed their angered hands
And them denied the freedom to abuse
Great Lehi's spirit-heir as he pronounced
True words; as later other auditors
Mute would stand beneath the withering heat
Of *Abinadi*'s condemnation, and
Helpless stand to staunch his words until
From him the Mantle of the Spirit passed
And they—degenerate priests, unworthy king—
Proscribed God's Holy Mouth to heathen flames;
Just so were Laban and his brother stilled
While youngest Nephi unaware maintained:
    "Yea, think we now on him, sole son of *Nun*,
Who with the trembling weight of *Moses*' hands,
Who with the forceful weight of Priesthood's hands,
Received prophetic Mantle from the Lord,
Commissioned was to conquer pagan hordes
And put to flame and death idolatry,
Possessing soil once sacred-sworn to God.
Remember we aged walls in Jericho,
Round which the Priests and Covenant Folk of God
Full seven daily circuits marching made
Before *Adonai*, King of Israel,
Shook solid stone—threw down the city's walls
And access free provided Hebrew swords;
Yet even he in all his native might
And borrowed powers of Godly strength, yea, he
Who bore the pow'r and right of *Moses*' hand
Succeeded not at once in founding homes

For Israel's tribes within the Promised Land;
Long Centuries would pass until the soil
Was cleared by sword of noxious, pagan growth
That sprang unbidden from the rocky soil,
And God's true Branch could flourish on the Mount
Which now stands Temple-crowned before our sight.
    "Yea, oft have we of *Eber*'s trailing stock
Been forced to wait the pleasure of our God.
Thus is it now. We shall at last succeed
According to the Visions of our Sire;
It but remains for us to find the mode
By which we may fulfill a Father's will."
    Thus speaking, Nephi silent musing fell,
Nor spake the three with him in Council drawn;
None spake, but all considered Nephi's plea,
One understanding, two with stony hearts
Obdurate in their pride, rejecting faith
And history divine; though if, perchance,
The minds of Laman and of Lemuel
Were opened to the stream of future years
And they that could perceive which was to come
Their inclinations had revolved to God;
And Nephi's faith implicit in the Power
Of God to bring to pass His Sovereign Will
Sustained and nurturéd would be if he
Had seen far-sweeping human History,
Had seen dread Doom foreshadowed for his Loins,
As at the end, when Red had White destroyed
Except for one who struggled to survive
That he a tragic history indite
Of Ignorance, of Sins and of Truth's death;
Yea, at the end of Nephite Sovereignty,
Of White's survival as a Nephite race,
Had Nephi seen the Will of God succeed
In guarding and preserving precious Words
Which should to future readers be revealed,
Then Nephi would have felt the wrenching pain

Moroni knew, who witnessed Death and Loss
Of all that him of humankind remained,
Of all that to his hopeless Sight endured.
How often would the aged *Moroni* feel
The mantle's weight of his Celestial Call,
That Nephite history should be incised
Into the gleaming plated of alloyed Gold;
And in those Plates rich promises record
By which all souls should prosper in new lands
Or plummet to black Stygian depths as they,
The Promised Ones, fulfilled or disobeyed
Eternal mandates high; indeed, his ore
Reflected oppositions free for Man;
As Greek *Achilles*' shield his fate revealed—
An early death in battle and great fame
If he armed, martial pathways chose to tread,
Or lingering life and base obscurity
Had he his mighty thews and arms denied—
So offer bold *Moroni*'s Plates a choice
For Israel's weak Progeny; true Life
And Immortality through God if they
The iron path of Righteousness endure;
Or death, defeat, and darkness absolute
Expanding to encompass gray Eternities
If they pure Light with conscience full rejects
In favor of the sheltering shade of sin
And secret wickedness—yea, *Mormon*'s son
(And Lehi's distant, distant spirit-son)
Commissioned was to ingrave the Will of God
In earnest warning to all hearts; and yet
Did he fulfill at once his Stewardship?
Did he fulfill with ease his Stewardship?
Or did his labors span the flowing tide
Of fourteen Centuries before at last
His mantle was removed, to Joseph giv'n
In nighttime Visitation, as if by
A Holy Muse revealed, a *Messenger* restored,

And *Joseph* Joseph's-son achieved that end
For which *Moroni* wrote his father's words?
    Again, could Lehi's branches peer into
Deep-veiled futurity, to see the Children
Of the Latter Covenant complete
A Holy Temple to the Most High God,
A Holy Place constructed through the Sight
And visionary Knowledge high to him
Extended, and through Truth by him restored,
By *Joseph*, Prophet of the Latter-days,
Who guided sacrificing hands that built
A Tabernacle to the Lord of Hosts
In splendor rivaling that edifice
Bright-gleaming o'er stone walls of David's state;
Had then perchance dark Laman, Lemuel
More worthy proven of their Father's Name;
Had they but seen the faithful, novice hands
That struggled in deep Western Wilderness,
In Kirtland's forest calm and rural still
To raise a Tabernacle to their God,
A House in which Earth's *Christ* might come to Man,
In which all Centers and Circumference
Be circumscribed, a Holy Place, a Pole
Between mortality and Ever-Life;
A House resplendent in pink Dawning Light
As if inset with precious Orient gems
Upon a marble background pure, sublime
(Encrusted, truly, through the sacrifice
Of heirloom china, crushed and mingled with
White, spotless lime to clothe rough, hand-formed bricks
With whiteness rivaling Celestial Courts—
Or so near to as might be found on Earth,
Rival for excessive brightness of the
Sphere itself of God, bright Kolob's Sphere—;
For those who built in *Kirtland*'s sylvan place
No gold, no jewels had, no fragrant woods
From Lebanon, nor ores from *Solomon*'s

Deep-hidden desert mines at their command,
As had the Heav'n-Wise King who first upraised
The shining Crown of Zion's Holy Mount;
Or as those sons of Lehi's teeming loins
Who, in high righteousness, on peaceful shores
A Temple built to honor God, endowed
And ornamented with fine, beauteous stones
And rare delights profusely garnered from
The virgin depths of Western Continents);
Yet durst they not—those Saints of Latter-days,
Yea, durst they not there linger to enjoy
The beauty and magnificence of that
Which served as seat for *Christ*'s return in Flesh—
Nay, forced by ignorance and fear they fled,
Wandered through green, fertile plains until
Prophetic wisdom forged from misty swamps
The City Beautiful, snow-white *Nauvoo*,
With her crystal Diadem and Light,
The Temple; pure against a wintery sky,
White star-stones, moon-stones, sun-stones garlanding
Its smooth-worked brow, mute tributes to high ranks
Of Governors controlling movements through
Vast cosmic Time and Space in answer to
Informed desires of Heaven's God; yea, thus
Bedecked with stones the Temple stood, serene,
As isle of ultramundane calm amid
Smoke and flames demonic, terrors of
Morian flames, as lawlessness rebelled
Against true Order and Degree; foul Hate
O'erwhelming mobs as Beautiful *Nauvoo*
Pale victim fell to ravaging and rape,
To untimely, horrifying death
Of God's anointed Spokesman, Priest, and Seer;
Just as proud Jerusalem would fall
In Lehi's time to Babylon's dire power,
Her massy walls of stone o'erthrown and razed,
Her populace in rags and bondage led

Unto the farthest reaches Northward set,
There to serve in patient servitude
Until *Jehovah* once again should cause
Return to ruins which once knew David's Crown.
So it was then with Nauvoo's Peace,
As thoughtless mobs made desolate the homes
Of Saints from every land together come;
Yet breathed unsullied yet on swelling Earth
The Temple's untouched sanctity—when, No!
It must not, cannot be!—they desecrate
The House of God! Crazed windows glow blood-red
Where once suffusing auras flickered o'er
An amber Altar, and deep-roaring Winds
Gave Voice to suffering and hope; and then
Burst forth flames serpentine—consuming flames—
And they whose calloused hands this Godly House
Upreared now shoulder goods and flow across
Ice-pavements, seeking paths that lead to Hope,
Paths into the waiting, virgin West,
Paths into high Mountain Vales where they,
The desolate, might build again their lives,
Regain sin-shattered dreams, and Zion see
In righteousness and flourishing delight
Within the rose-filled Desert wastes endure;
And thus across the ice survivors fled,
The City *Nauvoo* given o'er to flames,
God's House relinquished to mad, streaming mobs,
And *Joseph*'s grail-tomb lost to mortal time.
    Yet once again, the third time, seek pure hearts
Persuaded by the Truths of *Joseph*'s life
To rear an edifice to God; in wastes
And salty desert barrenness they build
Foundations deep of granite carved by hand,
And slowly, o'er the span of forty years,
See Pinnacles arise to form arched skies—
Pinnacles of Stone that rise to sweep
With matchless majesty the clouds themselves—

Three *Aaronic*, three *Melchizedek*,
With one great golden Trumpeter atop
The highest point (though placed there not as Christ
By Satan's sinuous wiles, to tempt with sin
The Son of God to worship Darkness' blight,
Foiled when Christ-God did not Fall, but Stood,
Pronouncing thus: *"Also it is written,*
Tempt not the Lord thy God";
But rather as a Symbol of the Light
To Eastward Dawning as he waiting stands,
Moroni Messenger, in gold enrobed,
Prepared to trumpet forth the Coming God,
To wake the waiting world with his call).
    Their Temple is complete, the third, the one
In which all Heavenly Glories reflect, in which
Telestial, *Terrestrial* and high
Celestial Worlds reflect their perfect states
And give to erring hearts a pattern sure,
A pattern visible that leads to God; in which
The Lord may come, reveal His Will to all;
And though the Two had passed, this Third should stand,
A witness of perseverance and of faith—
Even if its living stones lie flooded,
Its high walls drowned in salt-tear seas,
It shall contain, conserve its sacred heart.
Its heart of faith and perseverance true
Preserve and salvage through ephemeral Time,
For unborn generations long of *Saints*.

BOOK VI

Nephi reminds his brothers of the wealth of Lehi's estate and proposes that they attempt to purchase the Plates; Grudgingly the elder two agree; Lemuel enters Laban's house to negotiate for the Plates, but through the cruelty and avariciousness of the man, the brothers are forced to flee for their lives

WERE there a Muse of Future History,
A *Clio* self-ordained to guard, direct
The minds of Heroes in just paths and to
Them disclose all that must perforce ensue,
And she the gifted *Sisters Nine* would join
In Life Immortal on Parnassus' Mount
Near *Helicon*'s inspiring spring, that one
Might call to her and learn of things yet hidden;
Or were it possible that mortal men
Might descend within the bowels of Earth,
Into the black-lit fields of suffering shades,
Into dread, bloodless Fields of Erebus,
And speak as once *Odysseus* had done
To blind *Tiresias*' extended Sight,
To blind *Tiresias*' vatic Sight,
And tempt with Blood of sacrificial Lamb
The shades of *Elpenor*, of *Anticlea*—
Dread daughter of *Autolycus* and source
Of sly *Odysseus*' own life—and shades

Departed of the famous men of Earth;
Or meet as did *Aeneas* threatening forms
Of heroes slain in heated battle-fray
Or first progenitors of his own line
And spectral shadows waiting for their birth
Unto a destiny Imperial,
Purpled with high robes of Destiny,
Thereby to learn the course of far events
Unto the time of *Virgil*'s royal Lord,
Emperor and Man of Peace upon
The marbled Forum's heights enthroned
(Unless retreating through the Ivory Gates
One false ascends, thus proving all but dreams
And fevered exhalations of the brain,
Not Visions true that must some day Become);
Were such alternatives true-viable,
And had the sons of Lehi seen such sights,
Then had they differently performed, perhaps;
But such was not to be, for Signs and Sights
Do always follow evidence of Faith;
Revelations, Prophecies, and *Gifts,*
Healing, Speaking Tongues unlearned and them
Correctly understanding—these are not
Withdrawn, nor do they dwindle from the Earth
Except as hearts from righteous paths depart
And know not God, in Whom their trust should be—
Thus spake gray *Mormon*, distant scion of
Bold Nephi's line to all, to prove that Signs,
True Miracles can ne'er occur unless
Upon a fundament of Faith; which failed
In Laman and in Lemuel, and thus
Great Lehi's sons were forced to fall
Upon foundations of their human Sight;
And of swift streams converging far beyond
Their life-spans knew these sons of Lehi's eld
No branch (though Nephi soon, upon the Mount
O'erlooking *Moses*' Sea, through earnest Prayer

Would learn of Humankind's bleak future course
Revealed in mind-expanding mental bursts
As *Elohim*'s Anointed him appeared
To bring to Nephi's consciousness the shape
Of high Eternal Verities through Time,
And form in Nephi's consciousness the stream
By which his Progeny should flow until
The Coming of the Resurrected Christ
To Western Shores, to Nephite righteousness,
And these great Visions did to him appear
In recognition of strong faith applied
In life's decisions and strange circumstance):
Yet had the elder Twain full knowledge shared,
They still had murmured 'gainst the youngest son,
For thus it was their choice, and God would not compel
Obedience through knowledge granted them.
And thus it was that as the elder two
Considered their immediate surcease
From Lehi's will, young, beardless Nephi spake
To counsel faith-frail ones: "My brethren bold,
Since force and arguments direct have failed,
Perhaps alternatives exist that we
Might turn through diligence to our success.
Succeed we must, in Lehi's name, who spake
In Vision for the Lord; yet is our path
Through present circumstances again unto
Our Father's tents for our weak eyes unclear.
Some means must be, some means must here lie hidden,
Some Key concealed within the folded cloak
Of nightly circumstance and present toil,
By which we might obtain the Plates that tell
And bear the inscription of our Heritage.

  "Laman, spake you not of Laban's wealth
And treasures stored, less opulent than ours,
Than Lehi's precious things from lands far-flung,
Through perseverance, wisdom, blessings from
On High garnered now within these walls;

Have we not here fine gold and carven woods,
Massy silver chalices as yet
Untouched by blushed caress of vinous drinks?
Do not rich robes of Memphis hang within,
Next bolts of Tyrian purples and scarlets
From distant lands? These things are ours; and yet
No more, since now our present domicile
Must be the roughened tents that yet await
Our quick return to Lehi's arid camp.
Could we but strong appeal to Laban's lust
For sparkling gems and well-wrought metal's lines,
Perhaps we might thus purchase that which force
And questioning direct failed to obtain.
   "Quick, my brethren, up, arise; grasp
Those treasures most at hand, and go we now
Through broad Jerusalem's nocturnal eye
And enter to our kinsman's spacious house,
Purchase that for which we braved the Wilderness."
   Much murmuring accompanied Nephi's words,
Stifled whisperings through Laman's lips
And Lemuel's, to whom their Father's wealth
Too heart-felt was to basely trade for Plates
Of lowly Brass no matter how compelled
By Lehi's need (or better said for both,
By Lehi's senile maunderings and self-
Apparent need); yet strong was Nephi's power,
And stronger yet than Nephi's arguments
Were Laman's fear and Lemuel's of him
Who in the desert waited their return
Deep-seated fear that neither would admit,
Inwardly or outwardly admit;
For notwithstanding boasting words and high
Forth-spewed from Laman's mouth before the Gates
Of dark Jerusalem, yet trembled he
Before the imagined wrath of Lehi's tongue
Should sons return without the Brazen Plates,
And should to the blame imputed be

To him, the Eldest and the Chosen Heir.
    Yea, therefore spake not Laman haughty words
In opposition to young Nephi's plan,
Words that crept in unopposéd ire
Into his barren mind; and thus were bowed
And cowered the elder twain before his faith;
Thus ere long moments passed, four men-forms moved
Through desert air beneath the City's Gates,
The last and beardless figure leading down
Dim, narrow streets a silent, laden beast,
With grey-swathed, swaying, shapeless bundles bound
By hempen cords, covered from the sight
Of peering night by canvas coarse and rude
Lest subtle gleamings from red dragon-ore,
Or silky shimmerings, or pungent wisps
Out-breathed from carven caskets rich
With ebony inlaid and ivory smooth—
Lest these bewray to watching, shadowed forms
Close-hidden opulence progressing through
Dark, night-veiled ways in *David*'s capital;
Just so were sacred articles once bound
As Israel set forth upon her trek,
Resuming her nomadic wanderings
As years passed by, and *Aaron* with his sons—
His Priesthood-bearing sons of temporal things—
Prepared all Holy Secrets for transport:
The Ark of Testimony, wrapped with care
Within the ætherial Veil of the Lord,
Or that high Table (once by *David* sought
To ease great hunger's pangs with holy bread
As now in Latter-Days is holy bread
Made consecrate by spirit-heirs to power
Through *Aaron* held, and water pure, to ease
Sore pangs of Spirit's Hunger and of Thirst
In weekly renaissance of Covenants
First contracted at the cleansing waters' fount) —
Just so to that high table consecrate

Seemed Lehi's treasured mass, David's table
Soft-covered with a woven cloth of blue,
Or implements of gold beneath a cloth
Dyed scarlet-deep, concealed from human eyes,
Or ashless glories of the Altar hidden
By coverings of Imperial purple-hue;
And all securely bound by thicker wraps,
Badger-skins prepared by *Aaron*'s hands
To tight enclose such precious treasures from
All unordained or uninitiate eyes
And thus preserve God's Temple's sanctity
And sacredness inviolate defend,
Lest any looking be tempted to touch
And suffer as *Uzziah* did when he
At Chidon's threshing floor stretched forth his hand
To steady burnished gold—and died beneath
High-kindled anger of the Lord of Hosts.
    Thus carefully the four trod silent streets
Until the storied House of Laban's pride
Many-walled and opal-white against
Heaven's blue-black dome, the star-filled Canopy
Suspended glistening o'er Earth's sleeping still—
The house loomed opal-white above old stones
Of dark Jerusalem as Nephi, Sam,
Laman, and Lemuel near approached
To treat with Laban for the Plates of Brass.
Three remained without, concealed in shade,
While Lemuel, at Laman's harsh bequest
And in his role as Lehi's second-born,
Into his kinsman's home with quaking heart
And failing breath his way betook. Almost
It seemed that Laban knew his mind, knew that
Aged Lehi's sons should soon return, renew
Their quest to gain the Plates, for servants met
Sly Lemuel at Laban's Gates, conduced
Him with petty graciousness within, there
To confront Laban's baleful greed and wrath.

"Well met, my kinsman," spake the elder man,
His bulky frame rich-garbed in finest weaves
Of nighttime-wear, gauzy, airy, light;
Yet it opposition roiled his voice,
His throaty voice compelling in its ire,
Compelling in its tone imperative,:
"Well met, bold kinsman. Once again I host
A son of Lehi in my home this eve;
And do you come as Laman earlier did,
Demanding in his youthful lust the Plates
Entrusted me as Elder of the Tribe?"
His rumbling query lingered on damp air
(Damp night air scented with rich fragrances
And vapors cooling from exotic leaves
And petals floating in near basins sweet,
Attar of Roses, hyacinths, and lush
Green cedar boughs exuding fragrances),
And died into the heavy silence of
A chamber thickly hung with precious silks;
Nor dared faint Lemuel to break this still
And deign response to Laban's harsh demand.
    Moments passed as Laban mutely stood,
Surveying his unbidden. nocturnal guest;
Until with startling suddenness he moved,
Allowed his corpulence to settle deep
Into the fragrant cushions of a chair,
Scarlet cushions on a cloth-gold chair,
Its cedar arms of intricate design—
With florals, arabesques—by craftsmen carved
Who knew to create seeming life from wood,
To counterfeit *Adonai*'s generative powers;
A throne-like seat, in which ensconced the bulk
Of Laban seemed more regal, more a king,
Above all rugs and cushions elevated
With which the room so richly furnished hung.
He raised his glowing eyes to Lemuel,
And spake, his words compacting as they pressed

Between tight-smiling lips: "Young man,
You waste my time and me disturb from rest.
My age, my wealth demand respect from you;
Yet twice since God's great candle westward set
Have sons of Lehi, scions of a man
Who wildly prophesies impending Doom
And martial consequence for Israel's heirs—
Yea, twice are come within these private walls
Intruders for this same unthinking stock.
What would you have of me! Speak, I say!"
  With sullen cringing shuffle, Lemuel
Approached apace, to stand before the man,
Cowed by Laban's words, by Laban's powers,
And forced by will superior to speak
Even though his lips could frame no sound
Immediate but needed space of breath
In preparation for his halting words;
The younger op'd his mouth and slowly said:
"Sir, with great regret I come this night,
Ne'er thinking to have bothered your repose;
But high desires parental must be served,
For well you know *Adonai*'s sovereign will,
That parents must be honored and obeyed
Above all laws ephemeral of man,
Of state, of kings; the laws of God alone
Precedence take before a Father's will—
For this our history and traditions tell.
My father, sir, is a visionary man,
As you well know and we, his sons, regret;:
He dreams of flames, destructions, and of wars,
Which to evade he flees into deserts
With family, with servitors, with goods,
No more to look upon the golden brow
Of *Solomon*'s majestic edifice
Or sit in peace in grey-green olive's shade
Beneath the Temple's stony parapet
And look upon cool Kidron's cooling gleam

From balconies of our ancestral hall.
He would escape Calamities unseen
(Yet whether real or false I know not how
To tell); but one obsessive thought remains
To be fulfilled before he turns his back
Forever on his father's lands. He feels,
Nay, is convinced that he must know the line
By which his blood descends from *Abraham*,
He must possess a record of his name,
The History that tells us who we are;
Thereto the Prophets' teachings must be bound
Lest we (so he imagines) fail in sin
And die as fruitless, withered, barren stock.
Thus come we now to you (and *we* I say
In deference to those who wait without)
To bargain in our Father's name for that
Which he requires—the Plates of Brass.
From Lehi's stores we have brought gold, and silks,
And fine works valued high above base brass,
To offer in exchange for Brazen Plates—
Twice the mass, the value tripled twice
Of that you here preserve and here possess."
    At mention of such finely wrought exchange,
With no small profit to accrue to him,
Laban's porcine gaze intensified,
His eyes passed quickly o'er the gaudy room
As if to make accounting of its wealth;
Not did he fail to weigh the metal's worth
Which should exchangéd be for purer pelf
Unless…and here a subtle shadow flickered
In dark deep-set eyes, a sudden surge
Of animation played about his lips,
Unseen, unheeded by rash Lemuel,
Who thought himself a match in intellect
And cleverness for one such as Laban,
Whose treasures great-amassed gave mute defense
Of subtlety, of skill, and of deceit

Practiced on gulled, unsuspecting souls
Of his own race; this Lehi wisely knew
From long years spent observing Laban's trade,
But ignorance deep-blinded Lemuel's eyes
To wiles and ploys practiced by sly Laban.
Thus with high thoughts of merited success
Did unschooled Lemuel respond to words
Of acquiescence breathed by him who was
His kinsman-foe, for Laban stood and spake:
    "Full have I me bethought your offering,
And notwithstanding injuries threatenéd
Or real received by me at Lehi's hands
In decades past our current memories,
As lately by the intrusion of his sons
Into my lawful, restful sanctity,
Yet do I feel impelled to assent unto
The exchange by you proposed; but only when
Through practiced witness of my careful eye
I am convinced that I just weight receive,
Thrice-doubled value of the Brazen Sheets,
As offered by your mouth's unquestioned words
And validated by my merchant's eye.
Call in your brethren, then, call them inside,
Bring forth your goods and spread your treasure-troves
Before my sight; I in turn shall send
A servant to the Chamber where resides
The written records of the House of God.
Now haste, the hour grows late, and I would fain
Soon rest my weariness and soothe my age."
    With this he passed one trembling hand before
His sheening face, as one in pain or age
Might move with tremulous grace; nor yet could
Laman see the fiery glint in Laban's
Hooded eyes, not apprehend triumphal
Breath as Laman bowed, withdrew, to summon
Lehi's sons, to bring their offered gold.
As Lemuel with wordless expedition

Quietly withdrew from Laban's sight,
Exchanging brilliant, glowing, lamp-lit scenes
For gathering shadows and exterior night,
Behold, the guileful Laban whispered low,
Confiding to a servitor his will;
And thus the man, duplicitous and sly,
Awaited entry of hoar Lehi's sons,
His smiling lips dissembling, false, and cruel,
In eager expectation of revenge
For wrongs imaginéd, imagined wrongs
That led to death for his own eldest son—
Yea, now the time for quittance had arrived
And he would gain revenge on Lehi's House....
And not a little profit to himself.

    Soon entered through the open chamber door
Three sons of him who in harsh desert airs
Awaited signs and portents of their zeal,
Termination of their given task—
Three sons of Lehi entered Laban's home
(For Laman dared no more reveal his form
Or face unto white, naked anger of
This vengeful father of a long-slain youth,
But rather waited with the patient beast,
Now unburdened of its precious hoard,
Its grizzled coat a ghost-white blur of light
Against the shadowed niche in which it stood);
And as rash Lemuel his brothers' steps
Directed into Laban's rich-hung room,
Their seeming-cordial host stepped near unto
A jewel-encrusted sheath in which reposed
Unblooded yet a Blade, with blazing hilt
Of finest gold, new-forged for Laban's grasp
And his alone, for none save he had drawn
Its burnished length from jeweled scabbard rich;
Nor was the subtle movement wholly hidden
From Nephi's careful, ever-watchful eyes,
Though Lemuel regarded not vague hints

Of coming danger, so confident was he
Of near success and praise from Lehi's voice.
    At that moment, as Lehi's second son
Was bent beneath the burden of a weighted
Bag, back bent, eyes downcast with golden weight,
With one swift motion of a jeweled hand,
Strong fingers round begirt with flashing rings
Inset with crystal fires and flaming milk,
Dark Laban gave unvoiced commands that they
Who so invaded from lead-realms of night
Their golden burden should unveil, expose
To his unerring, estimating eye.
Scarce could he feign disinterest, scarce hold
In strict abeyance lustful stare and gaze
Acquisitive, as Nephi, Lemuel,
And Sam revealed the richness of their house
Which Laban had intuited, not seen;
Scarce could sly, covetous Laban stay his hand
From fondling with obsessive, eager joy
Fine golden rarities before him strewn;
Yet with main effort did he so appear
As if the exchange contracted were but small,
Until to him as spokesman Lemuel
Addressed his words: "My kinsman, great Laban
Of a House known far for wealth, look and choose
Among the riches here displayed for you
(Which may be yours if you but keep your word),
And choose the finest in exchange for goods
Lesser valued, lesser worth, Brazen Goods,
Which in his wandering eld my hoary sire
Has fixed dim, visionary eyes upon.
Bring now the Genealogies of Brass,
The Plates of burnished, alloyed metal base
For which you shall receive of treasures pure
Value manifold, multiplied, increased,
That we may thus conclude our vowed exchange."
    So spake rash Lemuel, approaching near

Unto his silent, elder kinsman's form;
Nor spake the waiting brethren from behind,
But watched with deep uneasiness the face
Of him propinquitous the jeweled sword.
Laban glared intently at his foes
Until the fiery heat of furious wrath
Quick-melting his insensate mask of friend
Revealéd bare a twisted countenance
Contended for by rivaling armies' force—
Torn between grim, greedy lust for gold
And precious things, and his ungoverned hate
For Lehi's brood, a hatred born of wrongs
Imaginéd, conceived when he who was
His son and heir was by the fell beast slain,
Augmented by this sight of Lehi's wealth,
By Lehi's power among the richly placed
And those whose influence and sterling love
Oft Laban sought, and just as oft forbore
As Lehi Laban's hoped-for treasures gained;
In Laban's weakened mind bore Laman guilt
For one so near in blood (nor ever heard
The grieving father Lehi's truthful words
Exonerating Laman from the deed),
As Lehi in his mind convicted was
Of seeking unjust place among the Tribe;
Thus o'er long years of deep-harb'ring vile hate
Were Laban's heart and soul consumed with fire,
With eager hopes for furious revenge;
As once writhing, Serpent-Crownéd Three,
Furies known, or foul *Eumenides*,
Pursued the son accursed, the slayer of
His mother and his father's murderer,
Ne'er wavering in their sharp-eyes watchfulness,
Despairing ne'er of ultimate revenge;
So watched the patient Laban Lehi's House,
Pursuing closely weaknesses revealed
In Lehi's elder sons that he might use

And prey upon to rest his angered soul.
And now were Lehi's sons within his power,
To slay beneath the protecting veil of Night,
Where none might see his satisfied revenge.
    Yet as his fingers clenched upon the hilt
To draw his unjust Sword of Execution
(After named *The Sword of Laban* by
Pious heirs of those he now proposed to slay),
To draw his virgin Sword in monstrous wrath,
Bold Nephi burst the silent shell of air
And loudly crying to his brethren twain,
Warning of betrayal, treachery ere
Sword's length gleaming slid into cool night
And threatened them with death, he cried, he turned,
His shoulder hard against the closed door thrust,
Forcing thus escape from Laban's snare
Before his cunning kinsman could complete
The web devised of trapment and of death,
Before bronzed bars were firmly set in place
To block their only egress into night.
This Laban saw, and raising high his voice,
Commanded those in covert wait to hasten,
Slaves to raise their readied swords and follow,
Pursue fleet-fleeing feet of Lehi's sons;
While Laban sole remained among his gold,
His precious things new-augmented through goods
Once Lehi's mortal pride, now Laban's own
By right of possession—as he thought—
Abandoned in the sudden flight of them
Whose forms and sounds soon faded into night.

BOOK VII

The two elder brothers, angered by Nephi's faithfulness, bind Nephi and Sam, intending to beat them into submission; An Angel of the Lord appears to the four, chastising Laman and Lemuel, sustaining Nephi and Sam.

DARK hours had died, absorbed into the Past—
Repository of forgotten fears,
Abode of hopes grown distant with each breath—
Since Sariah's sons and Lehi's mighty heirs
Fled swiftly from their cunning cousin-foe,
By grimly solid messengers of Death
Outsent from Laban's greedy, vengeful voice
Were hard-pursued through Judah's somnolence,
Were close-pursued through dull Jerusalem;
As four unknowing wanderers might seek
With manful power black Caverns to escape
When trapped in *Morpheus*' leaden Caves of Sleep,
Behind them wildly sounding booted tread
Of warriors weaponed by the Opiate God—
Just so did Laman, Lemuel, and Sam,
By youthful, grey-robed Nephi straightly led,
Wisdom robed in youthful innocence,
By a silent, vapor's wraith impelled,
Through Labyrinthine midnight passages,
Through the open Eye of David's Burg,

Into the safety of the barrenness
Beyond all retainers, servitors, or swords
Obedient to Laban's twisted will,
Entered once again black desert's wastes
To seek protection for their mortal flames.
    Dark hours had died, and now was rosy Dawn
Her welkin-fingers stretching from the East
Across the blue-black face of palling Night;
Through Darkness' perils Lehi's hardy sons
Had fled into deep, pathless, unmarked wilds
Beneath Earth's muffling, covering veil of black,
And in a groved Oasis sought surcease
From deathly anger and exhausting flight,
There 'til Dawn to pass the quiet hours.
And had the Morn a goddess truly been,
Aurora, pagan deity of Dawn,
Endowed with life and breath by Nature's God
And set as Sovereign o'er slow-breaking Day,
To paint with rose mild dewy-petalled Earth
As *Sol*'s great eye awoke from Night's death-sleep,
She had looked down from vast Olympian heights
Upon poor mortals stirring on this globe;
And had she wisdom as the Grey-Eyed One,
Or Justice as the long-fled Virgin-Maid
(Reïncarnated in the *Virgin-Queen,*
Or so would great *Elizabeth* aver
Through metaphor and symbol wisely used),
Astræa of the Aurum Balance known,
Whose Coming should restore the Golden Age
And Earth as *Paradise* from ills redeem
That had encroached through Times of baser glow,
Aurora would have paused in rapt surprise
At sights presented in a palmy glade
Whereto the sons of Lehi had repaired;
For of the kindred brethren there obscured,
Beneath far-radiant fronds in shadows hid,
Were two with cruel, withe-like bonds confined,

Pinioned by strong, roughly twisted ropes
That tore at manly flesh with villainous spite
Until no motion them with ease remained
Save still recumbance in dun, sandy shade,
Within a rock enclosure, cave-like, drear.
These were the younger—Nephi, and true Sam—
O'erwhelmed in guiltless sleep by Laman's arm,
By Laman's wrath and Lemuel's despair
As, safe from wild pursuit the Elder pair
In whispered conference all blame affixed
On faithful Sam, on untried Nephi bold
For calling close upon their hooded heads
Ebon talons and shrouded wings of Death;
With no concern for Laban's treachery,
Dark Laman and the cohort second son
Conspired with angered minds unanimous
To bind and slay true righteousness o'ercome,
To slay the innocents with smoking swords
As innocents so often have been slain
By evil's wrath and godless power, thereby
To bring unuttered condemnation on
Itself in just requital for the lives
So lightly shed, so lightly honoréd—
As in Judæa's land by *Herod* willed,
Or later, centuries later, at the Mill
Where children died that Evil might endure
A moment longer in its false-strengthed pride.
    Thus Laman, with strong *Rhadamantine* plea,
Beneath the swelling beauty of the Dawn,
His councils held with warring Lemuel,
To urge him to unnatural, bloody deeds,
And to his younger brother thus framed thoughts:
"How is it that you do not comprehend
The danger in this stripling son revealed
Who shares our father's strange propensity
For Dreams and vatic, visionary Sights.
'Tis not alone this recent circumstance,

This near approach to life's abandonment
Occasioned dually by pale, shadowed Dreams
Afflicting sorely him who should with strength
And wisdom rule his loins' posterity;
By Lehi's Visions as by Nephi's Youth,
By his unthinking credence placed in myth,
In Sights which—if they do exist—are real
Only in an aging, mortal brain.
Behold, I say, 'tis not alone this night
And its experiences, near disasters
Brought about by Nephi, seconded
By Sam, false minion menial and stay
Of Nephi's youth—No! a graver Cause
Do I foresee for fear, an urging strong
That these must die, our rights and heritage
As Lehi's elder to protect. I see—
Yet not through dim, amorphous figments of
The misty night, but rather through hard truths
Perceived clear-edged beneath the sun of Day—
That Nephi's favor in our father's eyes
Waxes daily, rankly grows beyond
All normal bounds ascribed to one who last
Of four took seed; daily do I see
Our father more rely on Nephi's arm
And might than on the power of those who most
Deserve—by right of primogeniture
And legal, primal birth—than on the might
Of us, the eldest in the family.
If this proceed unchecked, unstayed, how long
Can we endure as agents to ourselves,
Before the ambition of this child shall rise
And, as a blighting, killing, fell disease
Us slay, and our posterity—not slay
In sense that he would rob us quite of that
Which is the burning source of mortal life;
No, he will not slay us, for he prefers
Unjust hegemony o'er them who stand

In natural authority o'er him;
Yea, he would be our Ruler and our King,
He would soon subvert weak Lehi's faith
In him, and governance complete assume
Of all the wandering parties of our House,
To lead us and our Children yet to come
Into strange Lands unknown, that we may serve
With our Posterity beneath the lash
Of Nephi's scouring words. This I fear,
For oft before in Hebrew history,
In Mankind's history since first drew breath
Our kind upon this sphere of ashen pain,
Have younger sons rebelled against their lot
And sought high blessings, by law not their own:
    "First *Abel*, grubbing delver in soiled dirt,
Who thought through vegetable sacrifice
An elder brother to supplant; and when
Strong *Cain* presented Flesh unto his God,
Behold, so firm insinuate was he
Who earlier his leafy offering
Had burnt unto the Lord, that altar flames
Refused to lick red-blooded, tender meats;
The fire, unjustly satiate with taste
Of Abel's fruits and grains erst sacrificed,
Paid but scant heed to wholesome nourishment
Offered then by Adam's elder son;
As this Cain wonderingly perceived, his heart
Grew wroth with righteous anger's heat, and he
The base suborner slew in rage—
For which bold deed he was by force expelled
From Adam's sight, to dwell in far-off lands
Among the remnants of apostate limbs
Through wickedness from Adam's stock lopped off,
Through uncleanness exiled from the soil
Then homeland of our fallen parent pair,
From margent nearness of high silvered gates
Before the Western Garden placed as bar

To joys therein once tasted by our Sire;
And Cain's true birthright thus was forfeited
Through machinations of his farmer-kin."
    So spake thus harshly Lehi's eldest son,
Nor recognized he in his jejune rage
Great errors in accusatory words
Directed toward our Father's gentle son,
Our Father Adam's murdered son, he who,
To Laman's claims contrary, guarded flocks
While Cain, the elder, labored in the Earth
And brought his tardy, grudging sacrifice
Of green for immolation on the fires
To Adam's God and Savior consecrate,
Savior yet unborn and yet still evident
In Seed that roiled unborn in Adam's loins;
So was true history, and yet so strong
Was Laman's hatred and disdain for all
Who lives as sedentary farmers chose,
Yea, and so strong his rage at Lehi's care
To burden laboring beasts with grains for seed,
So strong his base conviction that the son
Who fewest years of life could boast all sons
Into poor sowers of coarse seed would turn,
That Laman altered history divine
To serve his jealousy, himself allied
With Cain and Cain's lineal progeny,
Jabal, man of tents and cattled wealth,
Preferring herdsmen's traffic with live flesh
To grubbing livelihood with toil and sweat
Wrested from the unwilling Earth, from Earth
Who once her Bounties quelled for Adam's sin,
Bore noxious fruit of thistles, weeds in soils
Ere graced by lush and verdant harvest sites,
And no more with spontaneous joy brought forth
The thornless Rose of Eden's unmatched Dews
Or ivory Lilies' spotless purity;
And once again, in shamed acknowledgment

Of Cain's rude fratricide, green Earth rebelled
And him no more with harvests prosperéd,
That he in lands far-flung as herdsman dwelt,
His red-stained hands to pastoral cares confined.
This easily forgetting, Laman drew
Analogy from Cain's deservéd plight
To his own cause; thus just 'twould be,
In future years, in lands of promise high,
Unnamed—yet in the course of centuries
To bear with righteous pride their high-formed Name,
A Name with *Freedom* soon synonymous,
America, both North and South, lands blessed
By God—yea, just 'twould be that Laman then
Would bring upon his head, his followers',
A Curse to Cain's God-marked skin similar;
For as the Lamanites cold murder practicéd,
Behold, their Lord them separated from
Their brethren-kin by flesh of dusky hue,
By flesh of burnished hue, that Light and Dark,
White and Red each other recognize
And distant hold their blood-flow pure, unmixed,
Until through Righteousness the Stain of sin
Removéd be from Laman's distant line.
    Yet this was yet to come, and now stood he,
So near to Abel's *Bane* in temperament,
With words chastising to great Israel;
Thus Laman to his listening brother's ear:
"So were high Rights and Honors one denied;
Turn we now sad thoughts to other days,
To later, as the mild *Rebekah* bore
Two sons to aging *Israel*; two sons
Came forth at once—yet was the hirsute one
Some moments elder, *Esau*, herdsman, son
Most loved of *Isaac*, who was Israel;
Yet *Jacob,* smooth of tongue and smooth of flesh,
With covetous and avaricious fraud,
In secret combination with the one

Who loved him best, Rebekah, dark conspired
To circumvent the Will of Israel
And garner for the smooth-skinned, cunning one
Rich blessings destined for the first-born son;
Through base deceit was Esau erst constrained
His Birthright high for pottage to exchange,
Then cheated of his father's choicest prayers;
And Jacob gained the privileged elder-lot.
   "Yet do their fathers' sins devolve upon
Their sons, and their sons' sons; and Jacob
Lived to see his younger, *Joseph*, dream
Of sheaves and stars which low obeisance made
To one unworthy of such deep respect;
Thus flaunted Joseph a father's preference,
Until the elder ones rebelled in wrath,
Stripped Joseph of his garments many-hued,
The gift of doting Israel's great age
Unto a son unworthy of his love,
Then cruelly stained with blood and rent as if
Clawed monsters of the Waste had slain the son
Whom Jacob loved; thus acted elder sons
Who sold the prideful one across the Nile;
Nor did this stem his high ambition's flow,
As he through crafty wiles in *Pharaoh*'s Court
Succeeded to a governor's degree
And bent his power again toward the East
To draw his brethren to the dusky land,
There first to live as honored guests and loved,
But soon as beaten slaves to labor long.
Yet when the rheumy eyes of Israel
Were soon to shut out sight of Earthly things,
Did Joseph gain the birthright for his first?
Or did his younger, *Ephraim*, attain
The choicest place among all Hebrew tribes,
Did he not play upon the sympathies
Of blinded Israel, to gain from him
True promises of future suzerainty,

That gulled *Manasseh*'s sons dared not enjoy
The status rightfully belonging them."
    At this dark Laman stood and strode in wrath
Beneath deep-shadowed overhang of rock
That sheltered from day's desiccating glare,
Sheltered body but could not for spirit
Angered by unjust desires provide
Quiesence, calming cool, and peace; nay, heat
Like solar flames consumed dark Laman's soul
As he continued with his diatribe:
    "Now once again I seem to see a child
Aspiring to powers beyond his right;
This must not be, my hopes for my sons' sons,
Sons yet unborn but surely sons to come,
Will not allow another to intrude
Between me and my Birthright high deserved."
    As Laman spoke, he heavy grew with wrath,
His face contorted by the effects of hate
And fear, until his rash, forth-reaching hand
Clenched upon a nearby staff, a rod
Of seasoned wood, that as a cudgel strong
Would serve in beating to obedience—
And beyond to death, if circumstance
Demand this ultimate—bound, hapless ones.
Nor wavered Lemuel, but full convinced
By Laman's arguments, and wroth that they
In their precipitous flight fair treasures left,
Abandoned to the greedy, gold-filled maw
Of Laban in Jerusalem; yea, wroth
Against young Nephi and the faithful Sam,
And hearkening to hissed venomous words so framed
By sable-visaged Laman, Lemuel
Approached withe-bound and supine forms to join
His lesser strength unto his elder brother's
To smite and bruise with rods the younger sons.
    Quick, vicious blows rained hard upon the flesh
Of beardless Nephi and of Sam, as they—

The elder ones—unthinking, cruel, and vain,
Attempted through their feeble acts to move,
Attempted through their febrile blows to shake
The immovable faith of those before them bound;
Red moisture wept from torn and savaged flesh,
Flesh transformed to grossly dismal shades
Of purple and of crimson where deep welts
Cut viciously across their virgin flesh;
Yet murmured Nephi not, nor faithful Sam,
Still trusting that of evil good should come,
That all had passed according to His will
Who foreordained the hopes and lives of men
(Foreordained, but did not speak Decrees
By which men should be forced to tread those paths
Determined by the Immutable Laws of Heaven
Before our Sire in Paradise erst breathed,
Whose trust implicit in Free Agency
Stands ever as a Universal Truth).
    How long the punishment had been prolonged
Before sharp swords were drawn and brethren's blood
In earnest spilled, to seep into the soil
Of Judah's Promised Land (as Abel's blood
Had drenched the Ancient's fertile, fallow fields,
Implantation dread of human Death
So soon to follow for great Adam's heirs)
This none could know, for ere the elder pair
Their foul designs to full completion wrought,
Behold, as scales upon the sightless orbs
Of *Saul*, beneath Heaven's high authority
Wielded through *Ananias*' hands
Would fall to Earth, thus clearing sight and soul
Of one who fought to crucify again—
By sure destruction of all faithful Saints
And swift disruption of the *Christian* Church—
The Anointed One, until a blinding Light
Seared eyes of flesh, and Saul, in darkness,
Saw bright, holy Truths to him revealed;

Saw, repented, and became—as *Paul*—
A chief proponent of religion pure;
As Paul was bound by ignorance and hate,
Yet felt the bonds destroyed by that bright Light
Upon him falling, felling all his pride;
So withered, snapped, and fell cruel cords upon
Sharp-crystalled sands, while Sam and Nephi stood
Erect before two awe-filled forms of them
From whose strong arms all power and life had fled.
And as burst, blasted coils serpentine
With slowly sinuous loops, *Medusa*-like
Slipped from shoulders, ungirt fast-pinioned arms,
And curled about the heels of steadfast men
Released from *Gordian* imprisonment;
Yea, as their tight-confining bonds were loosed,
A subtle glow invaded palmy shades,
Intensifying in its liquid gold
Until rash *Phaeton*'s hearse, the rampant sun,
Propelled upon its daily trek by Steeds
Superb—the sorrel *Eous, Æthon* white,
Pyroeis of the fiery mane and coat,
And *Phlegon,* he who bore the shade of night—
Until the Eye of Life and Hearse of Death
Was blotted, shrouded by the glorious Light,
Was as a black-scorched, shriveled, withered disk
Compared to unflamed fires within the grove.
Before transforméd, vacant eyes of them
Who watching stood, Light coalescent whirled,
Revealed a sentient form, in white-fire clad,
With shape and countenance Celestial,
Majestic and immensely powerful,
Yet manifesting deep benignity
To all who feared not Heaven's wrath
Or jealous ire of high-throned *Elohim;*
Though not so came to Laman's eyes this sight,
To Lemuel this visionary Light,
For in their shock-struck souls, anxiety

And fear waged unrelenting strife for sovereignty;
With such emotions then intensified as
At an aweful frown from one who so
Announced intrusion in the affairs of men,
Stiff, upraised rods by Laman, Lemuel grasped—
As bullocks on *Elijah*'s stone-based altar
Spite of drenching from sweet, watery tears
Flamed forth—consuméd were by Heaven's heat;
And they, the intrepid villains, were reduced
To stonied whimperings and mindless fear.
   Then op'd the Shining Messenger his mouth
To frame thus words for Laman's trembling ears
And Lemuel's (for Sam and Nephi bold,
Though near their brethren twain, heard not
Strong words of warning meted elder ones),
And thus with thundering tones the Angel spake:
"Why do ye smite your brethren with a rod?
Know ye not that God hath chosen one—
The younger of them here before ye now—
To be a ruler over ye, and this
Because of your iniquities? Behold,
Ye shall go up again to David's hearth,
To dark Jerusalem, and there your Lord
Into your hands will bring the man of sin
Who sought to slay you. Go! Obey the Lord!"
   Thus having ministered to erring ones
The Angel of the Lord approached the two
Who patient stood with humble mien, confused
At Heaven's response to their predicament;
For though dependent on their faith for aid,
Yet had not Nephi dared, nor Sam, to call
On Messengers Celestial to come,
To save their lives, their battered husks of flesh
That housed undying spirits that themselves
Lived and live immortal, through all times,
From raining blows and stinging, bloody pain;
Thus stood the younger pair with grateful hearts

For their release from threatened, cruel Death.
As Nephi and his brother Sam looked up,
It came to pass that Light enveloped them,
Drenched them with a liquid glory bright,
Transformed them 'til their brethren's weakened eyes
Could bear no more the radiance and glow
Pulsing from their near-transparent flesh;
Indeed, so white-ethereal were they
That Lemuel and Laman could no more
Distinguish Lehi's youngest sons from him
Who, low descending from angelic hosts,
Now spoke in secret intercourse with men,
As at the close of His mortality,
The *Chosen Son* transfiguréd would be
And in his Human-Godhood thus would share
Celestial speech, Celestial Light undimmed
As Angel-messengers unto Him come—
As *Moses* and *Elias* earthward turned,
Who never tasted acrid bitterness
Of Death, but passed undying to high state,
Translated and immortal (not eternal,
For eternality requires rebirth,
The Body resurrected, not transformed);
And as those three in sight of *Peter, James,*
And *John*—who held all Keys of Presidency—
Communed, a Voice was heard, the Voice of One
Who Earths unnumbered rules, *Elohim,*
Bearing witness to the Sonship of
The Anointed One to whom the transformed Forms
Relinquished their Authority and Powers,
To Him in whose sole Name all Priesthood lies.
So seemed this transformed triad in the glade,
Angel-messenger, mild Sam, young Nephi;
And though long moments passed as they communed,
No words could Laman understand, save those
Address to his unworthy ears along;

Yet could he faintly hear an angel-voice
That whispered comfort, hope to Nephi's ears.

BOOK VIII

Nephi, full of the Power of God, resolves to return to Jerusalem, accompanied by the others; They discover Lehi's house has been robbed; In fear, the others remain in hiding as Nephi enters Jerusalem; Nephi discovers a drunken man lying across his path, who, upon closer inspection, proves to be Laban, Nephi feels impelled to slay his foe, rejects the idea, but finally chooses to follow the Will of the Lord.

Now Muse, I must again my Fable break,
Make pause in this heroic venture framed
By my slow-moving, oft unwilling pen,
To plead for renewed powers of thought and speech,
Sufficient for the subjects I must broach;
For now approaches with inexorable speed
The moment when I, too, must bend my words
Away from scenes of hope and prophecies,
From visitations of Celestial Light
And life preserved through sacred Powers revealed,
To silent deeds so seeming dark and vile
That I would fain retreat in sorrowed still;
As long before, the sightless One, confronting
Human frailty and sin, spake words
Of tragedy and fear as he from joys
Celestial in Eden's Garden turned
To face dread scenes of mankind's primal Sins.

What tears he wept, blind *Milton*, as he saw
Through Vision's powers unflagging *Eve*'s sore trial,
Wise *Adam*'s tempted, tempered purity
In keeping higher, Procreative Law—
Both workings of true Choice divine in spheres
Devoted to the exercise of will
Within foundations of All-Seeing Law—
Yea, what tears wept, blind *Milton*, when he saw
And felt the rape of Eden's innocence;
And yet he was assured that evil's sway
Should not eternal rule, but that One Man
Would come to rectify Eve's grievous bite,
To satisfy sage Justice's decree
That Adam for his conscious taste must die
(For Adam suffered Death of fleshly mold,
Yet through the mediative powers of Love
Preservéd was from spiritual demise,
Enabled was to come again before
The crystal-flaming Throne of highest Gods);
And thus could *Milton* bear the heavy toil
Of speaking of Man's Fall from godly Grace,
Full knowing that yet greater Good should come
Through Christ's most willing, all-surpassing *Love*
(*Love* all surpassing save *Obedience*),
And Man as co-inheritor through Christ
Before the Throne Invisible should stand
To share in Godhood's Immortality,
That from damnation, saving powers should flow,
And sin—and through fell sin, Repentance clean—
Be thus revealed as cardinal to God's
Progressive Plan to people worlds with souls
Strengthened by and in and through Free Agency.
So might I be assured, thou Muse Divine,
That from the secret midnight deeds I see
And by this pen record for other eyes
A greater, better Good might new emerge,
And spreading moistened wings of lucent hues,

Lepidopteran wings newly unfurled
And newly spread in this ambitious flight,
Spurn that hull which once was home and life
To take its flight unto Eternal Spheres
Unfettered by cold weight of earthly thoughts,
Unwithered by hot breath of Tragedy.
    Thus I now turn again to desert ways,
And view from airy heights low human scenes
Co-mixed with glories of unearthly mold;
Yea, I now look upon a palmy glade
In which four men appeared, in which a form
Angelic unto two had ministered,
To Nephi and true Sam then framed bright words
While stood the shoots of Lehi's fiery youth,
Proud Laman and his compeer Lemuel,
In rapt attention held, without the power
To move or speak, or speculate on this
Eternal breakthrough into Mortal Time;
Nor heard insensate ears, nor saw blind eyes
Until a half-sensed Voice—concluding low
Its high injunctions to the younger sons—
Fell into silence, and soft aureate golds
Reflecting from bold Nephi's righteous flesh
Subsided as the Man-Form slow withdrew
Into a coalescent pillar bright,
Then passing upward, disappeared from view,
Releasing Judah's desert soil from Powers
And Light of splend'rous, ultramundane source;
And as the Angel rose into the Vault
Of Heaven's blue-domed Arch, the Sun, now low
Descended into Western, evening realms,
Resumed its pallid, blood-red, dying hues;
For with the swift return of him who came
From jeweled Celestial Courts, Earth's daylight hours
Expired into night, and silence reigned
Until young Nephi spake to failing forms
Of fellow scions of aged Lehi's loins,

And in a voice exempt from pride thus urged:
   "My brothers, brothers loved of Lehi's vine,
Branches gaining intertwinéd strength
As we with one concert obey his will
Who gave us life, let us now return,
Let us go again to Jebus' hills;
And let us faithful prove, obedient
To Him as well whose Word gave men their Light;
For He is mightier than all the Earth
And mightier than any frail worlds
Establishéd through His unfailing Will;
Then does He not in power far surpass
The arm of Laban or his servitors;
Yea, why should fear control our throbbing hearts
Before one man, when with us stands the Lord,
The King of Kings, the God of Heaven's hosts?
My brethren, let us therefore turn our hopes
Again to dark Jerusalem's high walls,
Let us be strong before the Lord as he,
Great shepherd-Prophet of sere Midian,
Once-floating infant on the reed-choked Nile,
Full-grown and wielding God's holy powers
Against all enemies of Israel;
Let us be strong as *Moses* surely was,
For spake he not unto the roiling Sea,
To have frothed waves divide at his command,
Roll back and form a path for fleeing flocks
And wide-flung *Israel*, that they dry-shod
Could Pharaoh's steaming chariot-hordes escape;
Fell armies of *Ra*'s double-crownéd one—
Duplicitous in crown, in reign, in soul—
Close followed, urging horses' flinty hooves
Upon warm footprints left by Jacob's sons,
Until divine supports withdrew, removed,
Allowed pent captive waters to descend
In fury on iron-armored Sons of Ham,
Who in their death-throes stained the guiltless Sea

With blood-red hue. Thus served the Lord His Folk,
Preserving and protecting with His might.
   "And now, behold, you know that this is true;
And you know too that one has come to us,
An Angel-Messenger, to speak harsh words
Unto your souls; can you deny? reject?
Wherefore do you find to justify
Your doubts and hesitance. Let us go up;
Our Lord will us deliver, as He has
The Fathers of our race since *Adam*'s day;
He will destroy Laban even as
His heavy hand of Justice and Revenge
Submerged *Egyptus*' sable warrior-sons.
This I speak, not of myself, but through
High knowledge extended me by the Lord."
   Laman dared not lift his aching eyes,
Still seeking comfort in the cooling dark
Until sharp memories of searing Light
And Heaven's majesty should fade to gray;
Yet spake he angrily in muttered tones
As wounded pride engaged soul-stabbing fear,
With fear triumphant, tremulous within;
And to his brother thus: "Yes, I have seen,
I have seen an unknown being, painful bright,
Whose voice has filled my mind with bitterness;
I have seen him sharing words with you,
Yet know I not the import of your speech,
But fear for me and for my primal rights.
You say we must return to Laban's house,
That God will there protect us and preserve
From Laban's depredations and sharp swords;
Do you forget so soon, thou beardless one,
The fifty blades that coldly gleamed as they
Us through night-darkened streets pursued to slay?
Do you forget so soon it was your rede
That urged us first approach base Laban's gates,
Within which even yet our treasures lie,

Forever lost to us and to our House?
Do you forget so soon...?" Thus hung his words
As Nephi's voice sliced through the thickening air,
Heavy with God's power residual
And with an angered righteousness fine-edged,
In-sheathed with words of reprimand deserved,
With yet unblooded blade of verbal ire,
Though not without a sorrowing, loving tone
As he reproached th'uncomprehending one:
    "Laban, fear you so weak powers of men?
You who stood within that Light sublime
From Heaven outsent, and have survived its flames;
You who have seen these ineffective cords,
Now withered, lying at my feet, consumed
With but a glance of His all-seeing Eye;
Do you still blindly thus refuse to see
Bright truths that God would freely share with you,
That should be yours through exercise of faith?
Then be it so, for He will never force
A human Soul to choose constrainéd good
Above desired wickedness and ill
(Counsel men He will, and weep sweet tears
When conscious thoughts draw far from *Kolob*'s Sphere
To dwell in realms unmerited, unclean,
But never force employ to thwart men's will),
Else were Obedience impossible.
Perhaps, in deed, you have your choice displayed;
Perhaps my hopes and Lehi's prayerful dreams
Shall little change your history. If so,
Amen. And yet I cannot acquiesce
That your resistance devilish and fear
Should stem pure, high desires of Him above,
And flaws allow into the patterned weave
That is our life and moves our destiny,
That we create through conscious choices made
And exercise of Agency divine,
Immutably decreed for sons of Earth.

Laman, Lemuel, I will return;
And with me Sam shall come. You may remain
Within these stony clefts, you may return
To Lehi's transient home, or with us come.
Yours is the choice, but I will not be swayed.
Though Laban us oppose with fifty swords,
Nay, with ten times a thousand swords unsheathed,
Burnished blades of unmatched excellence,
Our Father's wishes shall be met in full.
Thus saith the Lord: 'Return.' And thus I go."
    Young Nephi spake no more but towered in
His mighty strength and rightful majesty
(Befitting one who yet as King would reign
And Priest preside within the Promised Land
To Westward hidden, by God prepared for him),
That Lemuel nor Laman him withstood
Nor dared desire in this him to withstand,
But nodding gave assent that he should lead
Their company along dim desert paths
Again toward the Temple's golden brow,
And as frail Night her star-embroidered veil
Spread from the East upon the weary land,
The brethren four their tread, their faces turned
Toward the harvest place of Jesse's seed.
    Carefully keen eyes of Nephi's youth
Pursued the way toward the City's gates,
As he three elder men through power of will
Directed on scant, night-swathed desert trails;
One willingly and with an upraised heart,
Two grudgingly, with murmured plaints and fears—
Sam willingly, and with an upraised heart,
And pride in Nephi's strength, an honest pride
In his own strength of will to follow thus
A younger brother much beloved, admired,
Who now had worthy proved of all Sam's hopes;
Laman and cowed Lemuel with grudging
Steps, convinced by angel-force as much

As by their fear to wait alone while he,
Young Nephi, accomplished all their father bid;
Yet followed they their brother unconstrained,
Swayed by his reasoning and their despair,
Their fear unmanly of harsh desert stills
In which they otherwise must wait alone,
Fearful ever that a vengeful Spirit
Once again might visit them and punish
For their laxity, their cruelty, their fear.
    With diligence the youngest nigh approached
His family's seat before he slowed his pace;
From distance viewed, smooth walls of pallid white,
As cold, dead ashes underneath the Moon,
Gave forth an eerie light that chilled men's hearts
But that no breath of warming life exhaled—
Yet other light denied its golden glow;
Instead of living casements (window-eyes
Alive with living lamps and oil-fed flames,
Tended carefully by servants loved)
As a tomb sepulchral stood the house,
With blinded, darkened visage, door agape,
Door broken and with violence unhinged,
And without evidence of human life,
As long before fire-blackened walls of Troy,
Of ill-fated *Ilium*, peered down upon
The ruins of a crushed, slow-dying land,
And vacant windows watched with mindless dread
Achaian rapes and Priam's seed's despair.
    With whispered warnings to the other three,
Bold Nephi crept within two outstretched arms
Of courtyard walls to enter his dead home.
It was his home, where he in childhood joys
A golden age of pleasure had imbibed,
A Golden Age not long supplanted by
Gray-iron disciplines of adult fare;
But now no more. Its shell lay barren, cold,
Stripped of comforts furnished by wise wealth

And genteel tastes of Lehi and his line.
Nothing met his searching eye but this—
A moistly darkening stain upon the floor,
As if red blood in holy rite were spilled
Upon smooth-polished wood instead of stones
Hand-hewn and roughly dressed, receptive to
Jehovah's wonted sacrificial beast;
Yet whether blood of beast or blood of man,
Whether blood of friend or blood of foe
Was Nephi ignorant; without a word
He slow-withdrew toward his father's sons
Secreted closely near unbarréd gates
To share with them the ominous circumstance
And fear of slaughtered innocence or age.
    But gained the son of Lehi not his goal
Ere swift-disrupted in his stealthy path
By muffled cries and minute sounds of life
Beneath a dark-stained heap of rubbled waste;
To which young Nephi crept, to see a form
Swathed in ebbing blood, old *Gideon,*
The valiant, faithful one enjoined by words
From Lehi's mouth to monitor the wealth
Possessed by him who in the deserts dwelt,
Possessed by him who dwelt in desert tents;
Gideon, beholding Nephi's face,
With catching breath his hoary mane upheld
And spoke in broken whispers to the ear
Of Lehi's Sword and Heir—spoke of death
And thievery perpetrated on
The innocence of unsuspecting lives
Within aged Lehi's home, of Laban's greed
Which, sweeping all aside, consumed the wealth
And treasures of the house, so confident
Was he of Lehi's death in desert dales
And Laman's fear of swords and men-at-arms;
Of Nephi and young Sam, of Lemuel
Cared Laban naught, nor feared he their revenge

Nor righteous wrath at his insidious rapine,
Murder of old, faithful ones—yea, death
Of Lehi's men remaining there, for as
His blood-stained lips the source revealed of woe
And weary depredations seen, the head
Of Gideon drooped again toward damp Earth,
Sought the wine-dark stain that life-fires quenched,
Drank from the final cup that all must face,
And Death's dark mantle misted o'er his eyes.
　　　Thus grew in Nephi's mind sure knowledge of
Base Laman's culpability, his greed
O'ercoming scruples and just right of law
Urging confiscation of rich goods
Left unprotected by the exodus
Of righteous Lehi's strength; nor failed his will,
Though at the expense of blood in that exchange.
Such Nephi knew, as if a witness to
The profane deed, yet faithfully desired
Fulfillment of his Father's sole command;
His mind long savored visions of revenge,
Of enemies impaled upon his sword,
But such dark visions ceased, and he returned
To concentration on his given Task,
Leaving to the entombing husk of Night
The lifeless corse of one by Evil slain,
A victim slain by Laban's hate and greed.
　　　Alone into dim, darkened streets he crept,
His message borne to waiting elder-kin
Concerning cruel tragedy and death.
Unaccompanied he crept; two refused
To pass beneath the City's watchful gates
And waited, huddled in defensive shades;
While Sam remained behind in deference
To Nephi's guiding impulse, which proclaimed
That he alone should treat the twisted streets
That yet should ring with Conqueror's cold sword
Before the High-Anointed One should come

To bear His Cross of bitterness and pain.
Alone, unaided, sought the youth his way
Toward gross Laban's house, secreted by
Wise Nature's *Tarnhelm,* mystic, shrouding Night;
Deeper into Darkness' heart he pressed,
Drawing closer to his soul-fired Quest
Until his way was crossed by one who, drunk
With new-pressed wine and low hilarity,
Into the passage stumbled, reeled, and fell,
Face forward in foul offal of stone streets,
Insensate and undignified, it sprawled
Scant footsteps distant from bold Nephi's feet.
There lay the sodden form, its covering cloak
Besmirched with common filth and deeply stained
With purple from the grapy drink of death
That counterfeited dim oblivion,
That counterfeited healing, restful sleep
By fogging thought and blurring conscious life.
The man-form lay unmoving, drunk in death,
As Nephi near approached, cast back its hood—
And startled as a face familiar peered
Unseeing, eyes fast closed, cheeks red with wine,
Lips agape toward star-drenched, wheeling skies.
    As Nephi bent low over Laban's breast,
Not touching quite the prostrate, mountainous form,
A subtle glint of gold tore at his eye;
His hand thrust forward, grasped a golden hilt,
Withdrew it from its carved, protective sheath
Until the blade—as beauteous as those
Detailed so lovingly in pagan myth,
Blessed with names and genealogies
Them ascribed by masters of crude lore,
Blades cognominal, as famous as
The illustrious arms that brandished them aloft:
Hrunting Hero-borne, Battle-Lightning
Wielded against Grendel's Dam beneath
A night-black tarn, though irresolute and

Blunted by her scaly flesh a worthy
Blade for Beowulf, dark-doomed Geat prince;
Durendal, whose regal lineage pressed
From Roland to dim reaches of the past,
For Hector bared him erst in Troy's defense,
Unparalleled in splendor, though subdued
By arms preponderant and Achæan might,
Achæan might and subterfuge of gods;
Excalibur stone-encased, signal of
Great Arthur's fate; or *Narsil* of the line
Of *Earendil*'s heirs, preserved until renewed—
Such was the blade to Nephi's sight revealed,
Laban's sword unnamed (yet soon to be
The Sword of Laban called by heirs in faith
Of Nephi's prophecy), though worthy of
Renown, such was the blade that Nephi drew
Until the blade gleamed naked in soft light
Of coldly burning stars and rested moon,
Newly risen from sweet *Endymion*'s couch.
Staring at the golden hilt, the edge
Of deadly mien, Nephi felt a shock
Of power surging through his flesh and soul,
A shock of power unprecedent that shook
His muscled arm and shook his stalwart heart,
Urging him to slay the drunken form
Beneath him lying in filth-gutted streets;
But in his heart the youth denied that thought,
Shaping sounds internal, weighing thus: "Nay,
Life's blood-fountains ne'er have been released
By these still guiltless hands; or human blood—
For often have dumb beasts and wild things
Fallen under death-strokes from my young arm
To furnish thus the larder of my house,
The open table of my Father's house,
Welcome to all who hunger, all who thirst
And who receive there nourishment of flesh
And spirit's sating through my Father's words;

Wilding things and voiceless beasts I have slain,
But never man. Nay, I cannot slay!"
    Nephi drew his eyes from subtle gleams of
Gold, and would have passed beyond the place
Where Laban's corpulence recumbent lay;
But as he moved, it came to pass that on
Moist, dusky twilight air, a glow appeared,
Intensified, until a fiery form,
Until a figure clothed in white congealed
To thus address the tender, thoughtful youth:
    "Nephi, there sleeps Laban, coarse and drunk,
Insensate in vile filth by his own mouth
Spewed forth, as evil from his soul spews forth
To infest this fertile place. Behold,
Thy Lord delivers him to thee, into
Thy waiting, worthy hands. Therefore, stay,
Possess his Sword, and slay this wicked one.
This is the Lord's command to thee, by me
Expressed at His command, O Lehi's child."
    Nephi turned to look again upon
The senseless man, now bathed in silvered light;
And as he stood, contending with himself,
From swirling *Stygian* darkness' depths anon,
A Second Voice soft sounded in his mind
(Though shape and form it did not counterfeit
Of Being tangible, nor yet would Nephi's
Palm have felt a febrile touch had it dared
Assume angelic shape and stretch its hand
To touch the youth's in ritual response),
A Second Voice sounded as in his mind,
A pleasing, soothing Voice that calmed his heart
And stilled his throbbing breast. It spoke to him:
    "Nephi, young Nephi, son and heir-to-be
Of wise Lehi, give heed. Think upon
Those cherished laws so long preserved by plates
Of stone upon *Sinai*'s holy heights ingraved;
Did not wise Moses strict injunction make

Against the man who mortal blood would shed.
Think, my rash young friend: Has Heaven's God
So hardened in his vague immensity
That he could wish a prophet's guiltless son
To stain his soul with murder foully done?
Remember Sinai's Shepherd-Priest, whose hands
Were stained with Egypt's dusky red-blood flow,
As he in anger slew the overseer
In sight of laboring Hebrew-bondsmen's eyes;
And for that heinous crime he was condemned
By God's decree to view the Promised Land
From *Nebo*'s heights, but ne'er to enter in.
Forebear, young Nephi, human life to take."

Thus spake the Voice insinuate within
Bold Nephi's mind, voice serpentine and smooth,
Convincing in its subtlety, to which
The Shining One with chosen words replied:
"Tis true, that Moses angered slew a man,
And for that crime lost favor with the Lord;
Yet think again upon his ministry
And death by his decree administered;
Did he not plague dark sons of *Ham* with death,
That all sons firstborn in blue Nile's broad land
At midnight hour expired, and *Pharaoh*'s heart
Was softened to allow the Exodus;
And did not Moses' touch upon the Sea
Release tight-pinioned watery walls, that they
Perforce did drown pursuing *Memphian* might...."

"Before the Law!" the Voice in anger cried,
"Before the Law proscribing Murder came
From *Sinai*'s burning summit to that folk
Escaping base Egyptian servitude;
Before the Law proscribing Murder did
These acts occur at Moses' bloody hand;
And there your argument prevails not
In clarifying present circumstance."

Then once again the Shining Spirit spake:

"Nor does your initial statement stand;
For Moses slew the overseer before
Receiving Power at Jethro's aging hands.
Yet if you so require that we as proofs
From matters subsequent to Moses' stay
On Sinai's holy crest, and his return
To Israel's camp, examples manifest,
So shall it be: Remember then the fate
Of *Korah,* son of *Izhar* of the line
Of Levi's priestly clan, who with bent sons
Of *Eliab,* of *On,* and *Abiram*
Rebelled against the right of Moses' Law,
Who with proud Princes of the Assembly rose
To stand defiant to the Prophet's words—
And when they offered incense in their fires
Before the Tabernacle doors, behold, the Lord
Was wroth and entered to His Holy Place
To speak in Moses' ear; and Moses spake
Unto rebellious ones Jehovah's Will;
Deep sands beneath their desecrating feet
Recoiled from tread of wickedness,
Split asunder, swallowing that Crew
With *Korah* in rebellious death allied,
By Moses slain, at God's express command."
    As Nephi pondering stood, the Voice replied
To this defense, and thus with scoffing words:
"Again, you fool, you fail to satisfy;
For Moses slew not Korah's valiant host—
No man can cause by his own mortal voice
The Earth to quake and break and swallow men.
Again you fail to prove that He by you
Termed God has e'er condoned the wanton death
Of one man by another fellow-soul."
    At these brave words in high defiance flung.
The White One turned away from Nephi's form
To peer into thick, darkened air from whence
The Voice its velvet tones impelled;

Yet did clear emanating rays dispel
No midnight shade, but as the brightness met
Black night, waves of darkness deeper roiled
Until they seemed a gaping great abyss
To which no Light would seeming penetrate;
And to the Voice of the Abyss he spake,
His voice Celestial ringing firm and clear:
    "Would you demand that God defend His Laws,
You who know the consequence of hate
And disobedience; then be it so.
The Chronicle of Israel will prove
To Nephi's mind the righteousness of that
Which God through me demands of him this night.
    "As Moses from high Sinai's Mount returned,
What sight offended eyes to Gods attuned?
He saw in Israel's camp lasciviousness,
Idolatry, and immorality;
And in his anger separated he
Men innocent from guilty hosts condemned,
And with stern words from his own mouth decreed
The cankerous growth by death extirpate be;
By his command, delivered in God's Name,
Priest-Sons of Levi slew by sword of men
Three thousand in combinéd Israel,
Three thousand souls that fell as autumn leaves
Crisped, dry, and lifeless fall to moldering earth,
That their diseaséd souls should not infect
The righteousness of Abraham's blessed seed.
    "Nor did alone the Shepherd-Prince destroy
Massed enemies malevolent to God,
To *Eber*'s children's high inheritance,
As *Joshua* Jordan's watery barriers crossed,
To face the fortressed sight of Jericho,
Swift word went forth that all within must die,
Save her, the harlot *Rahab*, and her house;
Nor did the son of Nun refuse to slay
That greedy son of Judah's loins who stole

High-interdicted things and thus red wrath
Supreme of Israel's God called down upon
All wandering Tribes until the guilty one
Swift retribution met at Joshua's word.
Need I say more; must I describe the fates
Of one and thirty heathen kings dispatched
By Joshua at God's command; must I
Relate the tragedy of *Sisera*,
Who died in pain beneath *Jael*'s woman-hand;
Or should I speak yet of *Philistia*'s Bane,
Who in his agony God's foes consumed
By pulling down upon their jesting heads
Gray, massy stones of *Dagon*'s edifice?"
  The Messenger ceased speaking; from Death's heart,
From that black, deep Abyss a flash of light
Appeared to pulse, intensify, until
Before the startled eyes of Lehi's heir
(Heir in Priesthood might and faithfulness
If not in things material and rich),
A second figure, light engrossed, seemed there
In night-time's calm. A form majestic flamed
(If form there were, beyond imagined forms
To people Nephi's confusion, his strong
Desire to know the Will of God from will
Of man)—a form perceived majestic flamed
With blinding brightness, thunderous forehead broad
And on its brow a crown of jewels rare,
That flashed their scarlets, purples, emerald fires
As if alive. The fell King slowly moved
Until above mute Nephi's head; then stood,
His Voice a lion's roar, a rushing wind;
His eyes deep-set and black were glowing coals,
Anthracitic flecks not yet aflame,
Awaiting ire's incendiary heat
To kindle living fire. And thus he spake:
"Rash youth! be not persuaded to this deed!
That King, whose humble messenger I am,

Is not the Lord of Death, but of full Life;
This other one would lead you into sin,
As one persuaded Adam's noble son
To invite Death into your new-formed world.
More potent still this argument: That man
To whom you look in never-failing hope,
The anointed one (so-called) your father
Seems to see in future centuries;
He, too, shall die a wasted, futile death
And join those death-bound souls, *all* death-bound souls,
That in eternal darkness blinded dwell;
And his much-vaunted mission shall decay
To prove your father and your *'prophets'* false—
And this because wise Jews shall urge the Law,
Shall argue as this counterfeit has done,
That one man's life of lesser value is
Than man's collective life as Chosen Race.
If you do murder on this supine form,
On this form unwary, innocent,
You shall be one with those who slay their Gods!"
    Then pulsed more violently black-livid fire
Emitted by the kingly form, who seemed
To expand into dark, elemental night,
'Til as a *Titan*, overwhelming gods,
Overcoming time and space and universe,
With threatening mien the Messenger compelled
Frail, mortal flesh of Nephi to damp earth;
And would have forced obedience as well
(Or tried, to full extent of spirit's power
Converging on the massy weight of flesh),
Had not the other severed with soft words
Murky powers exerted on Lehi's son:
    "Nephi, listen well. 'Tis true, as this
Infernal seeming-angel would declare,
That *Christ* shall die—nay, must!—to bring to pass
His Ministry of Love Celestial;
Yet thereby shall His Mission High succeed,

For through His Passage into Death's domain
And out again into green worlds of light,
He shall provide Eternal Life for all
Of sinning Adam's mortal progeny;
And how shall wandering Lehi's House be taught
To seek and to revere God's Holy One
Without the knowledge on those Plates inscribed
Now in the keeping of this man you see.
Nephi, this is Truth: This is God's Word.
Now choose, for agency is granted men
To act according to their conscious wills."
    Nephi raised his head, perused two forms
Above him in their liquid shafts of Light;
Identical they seemed, except the brow
Of one with diadems was richly dight
And threatened wrath and anger's blackest force
Beneath its weight of gems imperial
Gleaming coldly in their Crown of Iron.
Unthinking, Nephi struggled to his feet,
Boldly stood in blinding, living Light,
And with full power of voice and mortal tongue
Commanded that fell, pale, and jeweled king,
Erst burst from circled bonds of blackest deep:
"I, Nephi, Lehi's son, of Joseph's loins
And lineage, command in Name of Him
Who is the God of Abraham, of Jacob,
And of Israel...in Name of Him
Who surely shall be born and surely die
I command you now: Depart! Go hence!
Withdraw your base, reflected, borrowed Light
(From His purloined who is the Lord of Light)
Again into dark kingdoms of the damned.
I know the *God of Gods* will never force
Apply to bring to light His Will;
I know my father, that his dreams are true;
And thus I know your arguments are lies.
Depart! Go hence! I will no more of you!"

The King recoiled, convicted by the Name
Invoked by Lehi's son, transfixed with guilt
And forced again into his hellish realm;
The blackness swallowed his once-regal form,
Diminished now to empty nothingness
(As at the dreaded hour when man declined,
Adam Father and Mother *Eve* declined
To keep a lesser law, in order that
The Greater Law bear fruit within the Plan
And Ordering of God, as Satan fled
Before the wrath and breath of Elohim
Into the Outer Darkness, him to hide,
The once-Archangel, *Lucifer*, of Morn
The Son and Glory bright, diminished, shrank
As he stood forth to boast before his court,
His minion-devils in dull-burning Hell
Of Mankind's overthrow and Heaven's defeat—
Then it was that Hell's unjust, fallen prince
Degraded was, his form assumed, that vip'rous form
By which he in rich Eden crept in stealth.,
The form by him desired, designed, and chosen);
Yea, emptied now to shrunken nothingness
He fled in failure to his dreaded Lord,
To *Abbadon,* Prince of souls condemned
Into Infernal Pits, the Lost Abyss,
And his loose shape dissolved into thick night.
Nephi lone remained to hear His Voice
Who, lessened nothing in His form of light,
Thus spake unto the desert prophet's son:
    "Live well, and in your valiant faith endure.
You have chosen wisely, justly, well.
He whose specious form you have dismissed
By calling on our Master's Holy Name,
He it is who lures men's erring hearts,
Lulls them with quaint promises of hope,
And gently leads to adamantine gates
Wherein all damnéd souls impaléd writhe.

You have evaded his deceitful wiles;
Now turn from views of dread Perdition's realm,
Look forward to the hope of Lehi's dreams.
There Laban lies; draw now his virgin sword
And smite him with your sturdy shoulder's might;
Thy God hath weighed the weight of this man's worth,
His worth self-chosen and thus self-defined,
Against collective weight of thy Loin's Seed—
The weight of Lehi's progeny—upon
His Golden Scales of Truth and rightful Law
And has decreed that Laban's pitiable mass
Of soul is forfeit to the greater Good of Man,
For better *is* it that one man should die
Than that a Chosen Line should dwindle, die,
In unbelief and tragic ignorance.
This is command: Thus saith the Lord of Hosts!"
   The Angel's words released a memory,
Recalled those promises first made the youth
Beside his altar near the Red Sea's flow;
Jehovah's promises that Nephi's Seed
Should flourish in far Lands unto them given—
Dependent on obedience and faith.
This Nephi's mind recalled; yet when he thought
To speak once more unto the Messenger,
Lo, all Light was gone, and he alone
Stood over Laban's drunken corpulence,
With Sword unsheathed, naked in the night;
Commanded by the Spirit of the Lord,
Nephi raised the Sword, a moment paused,
Then struck with severing might his kinsman's neck;
And closely wrapped in Laban's wine-stained cloak,
With sheathéd Blade about his waist begirt,
Nephi disappeared into thick night.

BOOK IX

Lehi and Sariah wait in the desert for their sons' return; Sariah, in fear for her sons' lives, upbraids Lehi, who recounts again to her the Visions which he saw and which compelled him to desert Jerusalem; Lehi assures Sarai of the safety of their sons.

MELPOMONE is fled, the Singing One,
Her goat-song mute and still. Come now anew
Calliope, epic Muse, with wax
And stylus to indite heroic verse;
Or pensive *Polyhymnia,* with veil
And sacred poetry demure and sage;
Or *Milton*'s Patroness, *Urania,*
Celestial Inspiration come to Earth,
Holy One; Nay! none of these shall serve
Where now my Fable leads—in desert wastes
Among dry, sturdy tents where Lehi paused
Beside those swelling Seas incarnadine
That once reflected slaughter to the Sun
As blood upon high torrent-floods appeared;
There, near the watery grave of Egypt's Force,
I call upon the Mother of the Nine,
Mnemosyne, mighty Memory,
To bring to mind the visions past, immured
In Lehi's consciousness; for as the days
Prolongéd were since Laman and the three

With him conjoined in blood and enterprise
Set forth to enter great Jerusalem.
Sariah's maternal fears grew increased;
Nor found she comfort in aged Lehi's words
Or in her daughters' confidence and cheer.
As rash *Niobe* lithified yet wept
For seven slaughtered sons and seven maids
Who fell beneath winged arrows swift and death
Downsent from proud *Latona* and her twins,
Apollo-Phœbus and *Diana* chaste,
In retribution just for grave neglect
By *Tantalus*'s daughter, purple-clad,
Whose knee refused to bow before stone gods;
Or as grave *Job* bewailed his seven sons
And daughters three, and cursed his day in speech
To *Zophar*, *Eliphaz*, and *Bildad*, ere
Daughters, sons, and wealth thought lost returned
At God's express command through Job's full faith;
So wept Sariah for her vanished sons,
So wept Sariah for her vanquished sons,
Assuréd as she was of their demise
At Laban's hands or in parched, powdery wastes;
Nor did she cease to chide her aging mate
For sending them unto untimely deaths.
And as days slowly passed with yet no sight
Of swift-returning sons, Sariah's cares
O'ercame her wonted reticence before
Her chosen mate; upon a morn, as both
Alone were seated in their sheltering tent,
Sariah to her make thus turned and spake:
    "They are gone, my sons; my sons are dead,
And are now bleaching bones upon scored sands,
Gleaming white beneath the noonday sun.
Thus truth I feel, as every mother feels,
Who pains of birth endured, and through the bonds
Deep-forged of love and pain will often sense
Across the intervening plains when those

Who are a part of her, though separate
By time and space, no more require life's breath.
    "My sons are dead—and this because of dreams!
I know you are a visionary man,
And ofttimes have your Visions helpful prov'n
As guidelines in our daily, busy lives;
Yet now I fear your dreams. Behold, where we
As vagabonds upon this desert pause,
Led from sweet Lands of our Inheritance
Into this thirsty plain. My sons are dead,
Upon a foolish errand surely slain,
Nor shall my bones *Machpelah*'s comforts know—
My weary bones!—that in a foreign place
Must rest interred when I depart this path
To join my sons in cold, unfeeling Death.
Yea, we must perish in waste wilderness!
My sons! My sons!" Sariah wept and chid
With plaining words hoar Lehi's Vision's Truths;
Nor did she silent fall until the man
Who her as maiden wed, who her as wife
And helpmeet cherishéd, to her replied
With words of strength, of promise, and of hope:
    "My wife, Sariah, you who bore my sons
And daughters beauteous, who in all things
Have proved your worth by amplifying strength
And wisdom, virtue and true joy in those
You touch with every moment of your life;
My wife, Sariah, you who share my love
Through years, sweet years, and sweetest years as one,
Loved wife, Sariah, amplify your Faith
In God-Jehovah through the words that I
Now pour from my deep-loving heart to yours.
For I have known you long, and loved, and now
In your great anguish I would soothe your fears.
Listen then unto these words I speak:
'Tis true; I am a Visionary man,
And for those Visions I will praise my God

And urgent Thanks unto Him consecrate;
For had I not far things of God perceived
In Dreams and shadowed Sights, I had not known
The Goodness and great Love our Father bears
To faithful ones on Earth; I had remained
In fey Jerusalem to fondle gold
And precious things, engorge myself with love
Of precious golden things; and there had we
Among our brethren and the Jews succumbed
To Death's pale powers. But through those Visions' strength,
Vouchsafed to me by God, we now are saved
And shall succeed to reach a Promised Land.
    "Hear me now, my wife and love; I shall
Recount again to you the Circumstance
By which I was impelled to flee unto
This Desolation drear; recall those words
That Prophets spake who in Jerusalem
Approached the anointed *Zedekiah* King;
Recall those words that from the past
Sound forth, as other men in other times
Approached the Throne monarchical to warn,
To speak to Kings of *Elohim*'s desires.
    "The Prophets long foretold that Judah's strength
Depended solely on obedience;
This message to renew was *Amos* called,
Isaiah, and the Seers by God outsent
To lead our People to repentant grace,
Restore our People to divine accord.
Often have such messengers us warned
Of Doom impending and upcoming War;
And as our Chosen People harkened to
True vatic words expressed, so prospered they
Beneath warm smiles of God's beneficence;
But when they have rebelled and slain the Seers,
Woe and desolation have commenced,
And thus it is and always shall it be
That Death begets but greater, woeful Death,

Obduracy of heart begets but Doom,
Regret, and everlasting Shame of Soul.
   "Now it is so in wide Jerusalem,
Now in the ears of *Zedekiah* King
Still sound such prophecies of coming Doom,
Loudly ring the threats of looming War,
War's thunderclouds but dimly yet perceived
Beyond far-distant ranges' craggy heights,
Prefigurement of deluge and of death;
Throughout stone streets in broad Jerusalem
Dreary lamentations sound anew
As *Jeremiah* publicly proclaims
The looming threat of high-walled Babylon,
The threatening might of *Nimrod*'s progeny
(Who ever covet bounties and rewards
To *Abraham* dispensed, *Nimrod* denied,
Though he, the Mighty Hunter, claimed the right
To Priesthood and to Sovereignty through theft
Of Noah's garment, Adam's Cloak of Skins).
Some months have passed since first he rose to speak
Before wise Elders in the Royal Courts;
Yet none would hear, for none are quite so deaf
As those whose ears are tuned to mortal tones
And filter out the Spirit's warning Call.
None paid heed to Jeremiah's cries,
(Save perhaps a royal, youngest son,
Righteous *Mulek*, whose propensities
Though yet unformed give promise high of trust
And care in God's desires, who seemed to turn
His guileless ears unto the harsh commands
By Jeremiah laid upon Earth's Kings;
And for this youth I plead in heartfelt prayer,
Plead unto my God, that he might live
And prosper in his faith, far from Judah's
Blandishments and evil, fruitless ways,
That his vines might curl beyond stone-filled walls
To sprout and bear in richer, moister soil);

Yea, none paid heed to Jeremiah's cries,
But rose to counter Prophecies proclaimed,
As did the son of *Azur, Hananiah,*
Who in this year of primal royal power
Conferred upon the King, appeared and spake
Against feared sights by Jeremiah seen,
And prophesied of Babylon's decay,
Imminent decay within the course
Of days or weeks or months at most, and swift
Return into Jerusalem of gold
Erst stolen from the Temple's sanctity;
And many credence lent to falsities
Thus uttered in *Adonai*'s Name, until
The Lord through *Jeremiah* spake, and told
Of Hananiah's death within the year—
And he did die, as we and all Judæa
Know and testify; yet still in vain
Did *Jeremiah* warn his stubborn fold.
    "Yea, thus stood Judah's state, in truth condemned
By *Jeremiah*'s wide indictment bold;
Yet he did not alone announce the fate
Of unrepentant Judah, caught between
Taut, straining powers of West and barbarous East;
Other prophets rose in answer to
Impelling urges from on high, to cry
Within a Wilderness of Sin, that they
Who in great pride inhabited green vales
O'ershadowed by the Temple's pinnacles,
Surrounded by strong buttressed walls of stone
But lacking Temple chambers in their hearts,
Lacking Temple virtues in their souls—
Yea, those who dwelt in proud Jerusalem
Should live to see their city uncreate,
Rubble crushed beneath a conqueror's Heel,
And they themselves exiled into the North.
    "Much I heard of this, and pondered deep
Those warning tones I heard; yet I knew not

Through my experience their truthfulness
(And loath I was to blindly follow them
Who confirmation had received, but I
Desired to know myself the Truth and Way)
Until a time as I withdrew alone
From crowded humankind to seek in peace
Communion with the Father of all Life;
I prayed unto the Lord in my own name,
And in behalf of you, my family,
And those who call themselves the Chosen House.
And as I prayed great marvels from the Lord
Were manifest unto my stainéd heart,
Were opened to my surging, seeking heart;
Before my eyes a Pillar formed of Fire,
Small at first, then growing to consume
The corners of this Earth, of Heaven's Towers,
As once *Elijah*'s cloud rose magnified
In cloudless skies to rain with fire upon
The Altar of *Adonai,* Israel's King;
Yea, as I watched a Pillar formed of Fire,
A Pillar such as led the Promised Flock
By night as they in wandering wastes sojourned,
A Pillar flaming, such as might be seen
Should *Jochin* and *Boaz* with burning light
Ignite before the Portals of His House
Who in the unconsuméd burning Bush
Unto man spake; and bright this Pillar flared,
So brightly glowed the Fire I dared not look,
Yet dared I not my humble eyes remove
From that revolving Light. And as I knelt
Before the Living Fire, behold, my mind
Was as a tablet smooth of waxy stone
Whereon clean Visions of my Lord's desires
With fiery brands incised, engraven were;
My heart, once stony, obdurate, now soft
And malleable beneath *Adonai*'s touch,
Beneath the living breath of God Himself.

"Much I saw, so much that mortal powers
Insufficient proved to bear the strain;
And merciful oblivion its veil
Between my eyes and Godly portents drew.
Because of that which I had seen and heard
Behold, I as a fragile, clinging frond
Buffeted by desert's parching breath
Was made to tremble and to quake, as if
My microcosmic form were subjectéd
To violent seizures in my world of day.
You well remember, loved Sariah, how
I came unto our home near Kidron's flood,
Half insensate, overcome by that
Great Spirit which from the Abyss unformed
Brought forth life through fertile, Godly powers;
Remember, too, that I uncumbered rest
Required, and cast me down upon my bed,
There to remain as if beneath Death's sway
For three full days, in body lifeless, still,
Yet awake in Soul as ne'er before.
   "The Spirit brought then to my waiting mind
And understanding frail such Sights that I
Might faint in joy them merely to recall.
Methought I saw high, opal Heavens part,
That I might see unto the Throne of God,
The Throne of aweful Majesty and Might
From whence proceed those universal Laws
By which all worlds are and shall be formed.
The Glory of His Presence filled all Space,
But to my unschooled eyes it seemed as though
At first I nothing could perceive beyond
A glorious, burning Flame of purest fire
That marked the Seat of Highest *Elohim,*
A mist of wheeling Light from whence flowed forth
A River strong of virtuous delight
That as a barrier, a wall of flame
Separated me from the central Light

Surrounding Him who Worlds of Worlds adore.
And as I looked my eyes received new strength,
'Til in the deep recesses of that Fire,
Methought a core of greater Light appeared,
Refined beyond all worlds; and He disclosed
Himself unto His humble servant's gaze.
Upon His amber Throne my Lord appeared,
Surrounded by all-praising Angel-Hosts,
Unnumbered congregations of the blessed
In attitudes of singing and of praise
Toward their God. I would have dwelt forever
In their sight; yet were my eyes then drawn
Unto another scene—it came to pass
That as I would into that river plunge,
More quickly to the other shore to come,
And there to bow abjectly to my God,
Behold, I saw One separate from those
Who stood in ordered Ranks about the Throne.
I saw the One descending from the midst
Of deepest Heaven, His naked feet impressed
Their sweetest form into the waiting Earth
That received his weight as if a lover
Eager for the press of lover's lips;
The luster of the One was as Day's sun
When highest in its wheeling circuit held,
At midday poised in its bright-burning arc.
And as the *One Anointed* neared the Earth,
I saw Twelve others likewise quit High Heaven
To follow Him who was their Lord and King,
And they in Brightness were above the Stars
That in thin crystalline intensity
Vibrating with the power of Kolob's flame
Adorned the velvet of Earth's firmament.
  "The One, the Twelve, assumed then mortal shapes,
Encased their light in tabernacles low,
Became as dust and mundane, dying blood,
And forth they went among the seed of Earth,

To teach of Prophecies fulfilled in them,
To preach and act in harmony and love—
And then it seemed as if I trod the Earth,
As if I lived in years that are not come
But hidden still within the folds of Time;
It came to pass, the First, the Holy One
Before me stood, and in His hands I saw
A book; He reached it unto me and bade
That I should read. The Spirit of the Lord
Upon me fell, and I could read the words
In characters of livid flame upon
White parchment sheets before me high upheld,
And thus I read *Adonai*'s sole decree:
'Woe, woe unto Jerusalem;
For I have seen thy Sins and Wickedness;
Abominations rise as rancid smoke
Unto my never-failing, sleepless Eyes
When should with spiraled gray the pleasing smell
Of righteous Offerings perfume blue Skies;
But nay, thy offerings are now as sins;
Ye have my Love rejected, and my Words
Through Prophets bold announced have ye denied.
Now hear the Doom of fey Jerusalem:
It shall be utterly destroyed by men,
And no more be a blemish on fair Earth.
The inhabitants thereof delivered are
Unto winged, warlike hosts of Babylon,
To die in vicious swordplay or to march
As fettered slaves into captivity;
For I released bound sons of Israel
From weary Memphian servitude, but they
Reject me now, their King; thus I deny
To them My Name—no more my *Chosen Folk*
Are they, except it be they once again
In righteousness and true humility
Worship me, their God-Creator, Lord.'
    "And as I read these things, my spirit soared

Above the mold of Earth, and I did cry
The outpourings of my heart thus to my God:
'Great and marvelous are Thy Works, O Lord,
Thy Throne high in the Heaven's shall endure
Thy Power, Goodness, Mercy over all
Inhabitants of Earth shall ever flow
As Fountains breaking through dry, desert soil
Sweetest moisture, waters sweet beyond all sweet;
And Thou in Thy great Mercy will it not
That they who come to Thee shall be destroyed!"
Then to me spake my Lord commands that I
Unto no mortal ear may yet reveal
(Not even yours, my love, may hear these words)
Except in part; for I was warned to flee,
To leave Jerusalem to Fate's decrees,
And with my family evade her fall,
That I see not fell Wolves devour her flesh,
Bare her bones before a mocking Earth.
Thus was my Vision; thus I flee in haste,
Lest he who shall Jerusalem destroy
O'ertake us in our slothfulness and we
Amidst the rubble of walled Zion die,
Surrounded by the blood of wickedness."
    With this, grave Lehi ceased his urgent speech
And sat in meditative calm, his inward eye
Again illuminated by those Sights
That had impelled the Patriarch to quit
Jerusalem and its high dignities
For sands and blistering breath of desert paths;
Not spake Sariah more, but she her tears
Slow wiped from wrinkled and time-withered cheeks,
Her spirit lightened by renewed witness
Of her husband's call; yet was her heart
Sore troubled as she thought upon her sons.
This sage Lehi knowingly perceived,
And setting once again his mind on Heavenly Paths
Exhorted thus his wife to diligence

In exercise of her brief-fainting Faith:
    "Thou, Sariah, art a fertile branch
On Israel's tree, a mother many times
Of sons courageous, daughters beautiful.
No greater Glory crowns a woman's head
Than shining Motherhood, when she may stand
Beside her husband and partake in joys
Reserved by God for *Queens* in Israel;
For in the act of procreative love
May man and woman share in Godhood's power,
By forming of the earthly elements
A place in which pure spirits may abide
Throughout imperative mortality.
Thy womb is fruitful, and thy joys are great,
Yet we must not forget that bitter tears
Accompany sweet smiles of progeny
Since first *Eve*'s Doom upon her daughters fell.
And not in birth alone do travails come:
Did our first Mother not despair at sight
Of blood-stained purity and innocence;
Did not she also grieve for him who fell,
And markéd by the Lord was made outcast
From Adam's family and homely hearth
As much as for her gentler son, whose life
Had promised much of love and faithfulness
Until so cruelly ended in death's still
Beneath his brother's bloody, brutal hand,
His hand who fled with stainéd brow to lands
Disgraced by sons apostate, daughters fallen
By our first parent's procreation formed
Before Cain and sweet Abel saw day's light;
Did not grand Eve, of spirits feminine
The choicest proven to generate Man's race—
Choicest of all spirits feminine save one
Selected to give berth to God's own Son
In flesh, and suffer with him in the flesh—;
Yea, did not grand Eve, primal Mother-Wife,

Deep sufferings endure for her sons' sakes?
'Tis woman's lot—and man's—to bear the pains
Of love; yet without love and pain were joy
Incomprehensible to mortal mind.
Yea, think, Sariah, on that spotless Maid
Who shall conceive the Son of *Elohim*;
What heart could not forbear deep sorrow's pain
That as a fine-ground Sword shall wound her breast
When He Whom she full nine moths bore shall bleed
For Mankind's sins—that He, by bearing guilt,
Might bring to pass all Immortality;
Yet shall the living knowledge bring surcease
To her who Son He shall be known by men?
Nay, I say to you, for I have seen
In Visions' prescient scope the Virgin's pain;
I have seen time's heavy lines engraved
Upon her lovely face, yet sorrow's path
Shall her more deeply press, for I have seen—
But speak no more. Know this, Sariah, God
Will bring your sons again to you;
Grave trials shall we face because of them,
Because of sons unborn (yea, for this too
Adonai has in dreams assuréd me,
In spite of our great ages' toil); yet not
As the anointed Maiden are you called
To witness cruel death and bloody pains.
Soon, thy sons shall be returned to thee."
    Sariah heard the words and felt a thrill
As Truth revealed itself unto her soul;
Her bosom heaved and burned with eager breath,
Breath tumultuous; the Spirit came,
And mild Sariah knew her husband's Truth,
And as her namesake, Princess of the Lord,
Awaited patiently her sons' return.

BOOK X

A messenger enters Lehi's tent, announcing the arrival of Nephi, who reports his successes to his parents, detailing his experiences subsequent to the death of Laban; The history of Zoram is detailed.

IN times long past was martial fortitude
Revered above all other virtues shown
And reverenced by the ancient *Vates*' Songs
Until blind *Milton* set at naught such claims
And gloried in the Christian heritage
Of patient heroism in God's Cause;
And he a prototypic *Samson* drew
Endowed with Wisdom and high Fortitude,
Fortitude of Will and Wisdom's Grace
Resulting from dire suffering and pain;
And well knew Milton of another song,
A tragic song of patient suffering,
Of self-consuming Faith in higher ways
By which heroic *Job* afflictions bore
Of body and of mind; now to these molds,
These patterns which foreshadowed perfect Faith
And patient Fortitude in serving God
By *Elohim*'s Anointed first revealed
As Christ within dark Golgotha endured,
As Christ upon Golgotha's heights endured
To bring about the greater Good for man;

Yea, to these patterns which foreshadowed Christ
Would I a third include to share with Job
And mighty Samson emulation's praise,
Would I commend to imitative man
The example of aged Lehi and his spouse
As they awaited faithfully return
Of sons unto fear-bounded walls outsent,
Of sons unto Jerusalem outsent.

    Nor was that joyous moment long delayed;
For scarcely had the pair their discourse quelled
And each reposed in meditation deep
Quiescent in their faith in God's sure Will,
When swelled a living voice with eagerness
Upon dry, sterile-breathing desert air,
And he who as a servant to the sons
Of Lehi in their youth (who last had loved
The valiant Nephi's infant guilelessness)
Approached his master's tented domicile.
He had daily scaled bold Nephi's Mount
To stand upon its highest eminence
Near to the place where Nephi's altar-stones
Crowned rocky heights, from whence his powerful eye
Far distant reaches searched for signs of life;
And in the golden glare of budding day,
He recognized his master's Equipage,
Into the desert rushed to meet the Troop,
And now returned to Lehi's stopping place
With oral message from the youngest son.
Thus unto Lehi's waiting ears he spake,
Rehearsing words implanted in his thought
By Nephi's own true-speaking, humble tongue:

    "Great Lehi, by your leave I shall repeat
Bold Nephi's words—for thus he speaks through me:
'Blesséd be the God of Israel,
Of Abraham, and of our Fathers through
His Seed, for He has led us through His Will
To high success in this, our Enterprise;

My Father, greatly has He strengthened me
As He supported those in Israel's past
Who were submissive to His sovereign Will;
And I have witnesséd the Spirit's Power
In speaking to the inmost souls of men'—
Thus do I from his mouth this message bring,
That you might be prepared for his success
And for his full report of what occurred
Within strong, fated walls of David's Burg."
  So spake the messenger with breathless haste,
Nor failed aged Lehi's ears to comprehend
The import of this speech for him and for
Envisioned though unborn posterity;
Sariah's breast maternal quickly beat
As she the message heard, for sure she was
Of safety and reunion imminent
With male fruits of her most loving womb;
Yet sat the pair parental without sound,
As each in silent meditation joined,
Deep thanks to render unto Him above;
Lehi for new-forgéd hope restored
By Nephi's hurried words of victory,
Sariah for return of her choice sons.
Thus waited they until without the tents
A footstep fell upon sharp, grainy sands,
Their tent door inward swept, and Nephi stood
In beardless strength before his parent stock,
A Youth, yet subtly altered by the gravity
Of forced events within Jerusalem.
  As Nephi entered, low obeisance made,
And honored father's eld and mother's tears,
He op'd his mouth and humbly framed his words:
"Blesséd be the God of Israel,
Of Abraham, and of our Fathers through
His Seed, for He hath led us by his Will
To high success in this, our Enterprise;
My Father, greatly has He strengthened me

As He supported those in Israel's past
Who were submissive to His sovereign Will;
And I have witnesséd the Spirit's Power
In speaking through the inmost souls of men.
Yea, my Father, I would now recount
Harsh trials and sore sufferings endured
Which brought us yet to point of full success,
That you might glorify His Name and Love
Who is our Guardian, our Guide, our Hope;
Yet ere I such attempt, I bend my knee
Unto you, Father, token of my love,
Respect unto great age and merit high,
Age attained and merit justly earned
Through Life's obedience to Heaven's Will."
    Thus saying Nephi lowly bent his knee
And true obeisance made unto his Sire;
Then there remaining bowed the favored son,
As one unknown to Lehi's eyes stepped in,
Who in his arms a massy bundle kept
Close-veiled beneath rough canvas coverings,
Of large dimensions, evident of weight.
Wordlessly the second man approached,
Knelt before the desert Patriarch
To offer him the burden straitly wrapped.
At this great Lehi stretched his hands to touch
The proffered treasure reverently,
Then guided with one thin and trembling hand
The weighty bulk unto the carpet floor
Where, with breath-stopping care, the agéd one
Unwrapped, discovered to his waiting eyes
The Tablets long required, the Plates of Brass
That should his lineage reveal and prove.
    Moments paused as Lehi the Plates perused,
Long histories consumed, and Prophets' words,
Until he that discerned for which he sought,
The line that branched from *Joseph*'s arching root
Through wise *Manesseh,* Nile-born, to spread

And reach toward blue-vaulted domes, to bloom
At last in Lehi's progeny anew,
In faithful Sam, in Nephi resolute;
As Lehi read these words incised he breathed
The sigh of one whose shoulders bear no more
Deep worries, high concerns; and thus he spake
Unto the beardless son before him bent:
"My son, my heart delights in this success,
My soul rejoices in the words, the truths
Herein engraved that shall Salvation bring
Unto my Children in a Promised Land.
I bless thee, and thy Seed which yet shall root,
Grow, and flourish in rich Western soils.
But now I wait to hear your chosen words,
To learn how your success was earned, how came
This cloaked, mysterious compeer to join
Our Company—proceed, unfold the Tale."
    And Nephi spake unto his aging Sire,
Nor hesitated he, but straightway filled
His parents' eager ears with careful words;
He told of desert travels, of attempts
Abortive to possess the Brazen Plates,
Of rapine base committed on their House,
Now barren, stripped, and inhospitable,
By blood of innocents made desecrate
While unprotected by true Lehi's arm
(As other homes should stainéd be with blood,
With blood of Innocents in Evil's vain,
Too-cruel attempts to stay the Coming One
From ultimate completion of His Task);
And with low voice and humble, painful mien,
With heart contrite beneath the Spirit's weight,
Inbreathed concern for deeds of death required
By One whose Will no mortal man withstands
Except at peril of Eternal Life,
At peril of Life with Eternal Ones,
He spake of Laban's bloody, deathly sleep,

Brought about by Nephi's unstained hand
In high obedience to Heaven's Desires.
And thus with truthful Words he soon embarked
Upon the path of final happenings;
For as the youth had fled into deep night,
Leaving Laban in a Pool of Death,
He soon bethought him of the enterprise
That had required a human sacrifice;
Then turned he once again to Laban's corse
And put upon himself rich armaments
And raiments of the dead; and so disguised
Began his searching way unto the doors
Of Laban's treasure-house to find the Plates;
As one before, within fey walls of Troy,
The many-turning hero of the Greeks,
Polytropos Odysseus, in stealth,
With noble-formed disguise (for he, too, scorned
Ignoble masks by Heaven's Fallen One
Resorted to, to encompass Man's decline,
Cormorant and toad and misty cloud-dream,
Then at the last a serpent enameled,
Gilded, upright serpentine, with devious
Coils to trap First Mother, slay First Father
Through taste of Fruits interdicted and denied)
So thus *Odysseus Polytropos*
Within the Citadel of Ilium
Whose walls of stone were doomed to aweful Fall,
Gutted by fierce fires of Conquerors
Expelled from the wooden Horse's sly womb;
Yea, as *Laertes*'s son stole through thick mist
In *Diomede*'s silent company
To bring unto the Achaean battle-camp
The holy, Heaven-formed Palladium,
Stony image of the Gray-eyed One
Without which his Achaean cause would fail
And ten years harsh besieging come to naught;
Just so the son of Lehi Patriarch

In disguise, bearing outward semblance of
A man both faint of heart and weak of purpose
But inwardly true Nephi bold and strong,
Sought that which promiséd successful end
Of his nocturnal stirrings through dim streets
In search of Brazen Chronicles concealed.
    And as he crept in stealth along the way
That led to Laban's strong-walled treasure-house,
Yea, as he moved within a shadowed path,
Behold, a figure passed in haste nearby,
And Nephi recognized the Servant of
His now-dead enemy, *Zoram* named,
Who on account of his great faithfulness
Was entrusted with one large, ornate key
(Not two of metals twain, as he would bear,
Sage *Milton*'s Lycidean fisherman,
The mitered Pilot of sweet Galilee,
To whom the Mighty One of Jacob should,
In cognizance of faith and love, confirm
High powers of Presidency thus symbolized—
The Golden Key to open Heaven's Gates
And blessings shower upon all righteousness,
The Iron Key to shut again and bind
Within Perdition's sway the profligate
Who *Peter*'s true authority denied
Who *Peter*'s right as President denied,
Until that highest Power by Earth was lost
In consequence of swift Apostasy);
Nay, Zoram bore but one large ferrous key,
Which key alone the lock undid that barred
All common passage to that place
Wherein things precious to his master lay.
This Zoram hastened through dark city streets,
The massy iron key secreted in
Safe folds voluminous beneath his robe;
Nor did he sight bold Nephi's dusky cloak
Until the Desert-Sage's scion called,

Until a voice as Laban's voice low-pitched
Confronted him upon his night-time way.
The Spirit fell upon bold Nephi's soul,
And fell upon the tissues of his voice,
And magnified his intellect until
He imitative close of Laban spake:
    "Zoram, pass you so with anxious speed
Your master, needing as I do your aid
And wisdom to fulfill my tribal charge;
Come with me now unto my treasure-house."
    To which the faithful Zoram straight replied:
"Master, is it you whose form I see
Concealed in vapors thick of nightly still?
For you I search and haste through sleepy streets
Of somnolent Jerusalem; for grew
This day to close, yet were you not returned
At your appointed hour from council with
The Elders of the Jews, and we in fear
And highly pitched anxiety began
To feel a danger in his black-hulled night;
And thus I was outsent to search all paths
Unto the Council Chamber's sanctity,
That I might aid you, if indeed required
By dire necessity—and now you speak
From shadowed ways. I await your words
And high commands." Thus spake the faithful man,
And through the murky darkness recognized
The stained cloak from Laban's body taken,
Although he could not see clear lineaments
Of Nephi's beardless-visaged youthfulness.
    Then spake bold Nephi, still with voice and words
Close imitative of base Laban's sounds,
His wonted throaty style of speech; yea, thus
To guileless Zoram's form the youth now turned,
Who in his quickly donned disguise yet seemed
To be the man that he was not—he spake:
"Zoram, glad I am, of lightened heart,

That you this night have made your way unto
The presence of my pressing needs. For now
Await my brethren Elders, near high walls,
And yet beyond barred gates' protective shields
That stout defense provide our city's wealth;
They wait and soon expect my quick return
With those engravéd Chronicles of Brass
That in my stronghold fast immuréd lie;
For in the counsels of this night we spake
Of ancestry among our House, and I
Was commanded to bring true metal proofs
For their perusal and their wise desires
Who would sit as Judges over all my tribe.
Thus I go now unto my treasure-house,
And I desire that you with me proceed,
For that is heavy which I seek to bring,
And I am heavy with the cares of Life;
I would sorely grieve beneath full weight
Of Israel's history. Therefore, come,
Lend me your stable arm and willing might
That I shall soon appease my Elders' will."

    And he, the faithful Zoram, heard these words
As if from Laban's lips, and him bethought—
When Nephi spake concerning Elder men
Without the City walls—that he who strode
Enshrouded in dead Laban's russet cloak
Referred to elder Jewish Councilors,
To Rulers of his tribe; and thus unwarned
Did Zoram lead the counterfeit who had
His master's form assumed unto the gates,
The barred and massy-portaled Treasure-Hall.

    As Nephi and the faithful Zoram stood
Before closed, seeming-adamantine gates,
Gates as stalwart-seeming as those that once
Protected fallen Adam's *Paradise,*
Lost through choice and higher Law upheld, from
Intrusion of mortality and from

Now-mortal hands that now might pluck the fruit
Of Eternality and live for all
Locked immutably into Sin's fell clasp,
So as faithful Nephi and Zoram stood,
The former spake, dismissing in the voice
Of Laban slain watching men nearby
Who guarded entrance to rich, golden hoards
And gleaming stores of precious jewels, of ores
Deep-delved from Mother Earth's soft-yielding flesh,
Then twisted, fractured by man's artifice
To serve haught vanity and greedy souls;
Red-gold eggs from deep within the nest,
The Serpent's treasure-heaped and guarded lair,
Watched o'er by an unclosing, careful eye,
Eager always strife and enmity
With the hearts of men to roil, should men
So dare to look upon their gleaming forms.
    Yet cared the son of Lehi naught for these,
But sought alone the plates of Brazen hue;
Thus Nephi spake, the other quick-complied,
And from a swirling, hidden fold withdrew
That Key entrusted him, and with the Key
Undid the way, that in they jointly passed
Through gloomy halls. And as they walked in stealth,
Dim-flickered light reflected from gray walls
Rich-hung with precious silks. Yet heeded not
The son of Lehi's eld these treasures' glows,
But spake undaunted to the faithful one:
"Zoram, come with me unto that place
Wherein are kept grav'n Chronicles of Brass;
For the events of this day fast upon me press,
My mind in wild confusion disarrayed
Now fails me in my dire necessity.
Bear me quickly hence and with thy arm
Support my age; now haste! our time grows short."
    So spake the close-disguiséd one, with voice
And mien so altered by the Spirit's touch

That he to whom he spake straightway obeyed,
And led the mantled figure through long halls;
Nor passed but moments more with secret step
Before again young Nephi trod pressed streets
And night-filled ways of vast Jerusalem.
Followed closely by dead Laban's man;
Through night-veiled paths they threaded carefully
Their way, Zoram burdened with the weight
Of Brazen Histories, Nephi bent
As if by age and grave concerns downcast;
Silently they pointed stealthy steps
Along rough pavements, spectral-white and still
Beneath the darkened eyes of David's Hope,
Beneath sleep-darkened windows, deathly black
And sightless, staring as two gray-wrapped wraiths
Passed without incident beneath the arched
And vaulted stony walls; until at last,
Soft-bathed in silver moonlight from a sky
Unblemished by the merest wisp of cloud,
In which fine points of Light Celestial
Rend the velvet darkness' canopy
To share with fallen Earth remembrance faint
Of purer, sinless Spheres, wherein our Globe
Was wonted once to share the blessed sight
And beatific Vision of that Lord,
That Lord of Light who all Creation rules;
Yea, as the stars their beams with gentle force
Down-sent upon a stained and sorrowed Earth
(Not to be cleansed as if with purest snow
Until His birth as Wordless-One within
A starlit manger lit by fragrant Star)
Two men strode forth toward near, rocky clefts
In which three elder brethren breathless lay;
Nor spake bold Nephi, nor questioned Zoram's tongue
The movements of his master's form—until
They came to a stone cave, from whence rolled forth
As from dead, quailing shades beyond the Styx

A voice with terror strained; for Lemuel,
As he stood guard, soon nodding fell, and slumbered
Undisturbed by waking fears; but now
With trembling heart awakened was to see—
Or so he in his fear bethought—the shape
Of vengeful Laban near the orifice
That led into his Cerberean cleft.
Thinking Nephi's foolish trial had failed,
That Laban came with murder in his heart,
Before he slow-considered spake this son
In fear and anguish, called upon his name
Who with him shared the cave's recesséd bowels,
Laman, that both might flee Death's gleaming sword
Imagined now in Laban's febrile grasp,
Though strong begirt around the figure's form
That now approached. Laman flew with haste
To Lemuel, and both would dash into
The Wilderness, leaving Sam to threatened death
At Laban's hands, but Nephi raised his voice
And in his native accents to them called:
"Laman! Lemuel! 'tis I alone!
Feat not!" At this, wise Zoram paused, recoiled,
And recognized the cloakéd Counterfeit;
He turned to flee, but burdened as he was
With metal's weight, he moved not far before
Bold Nephi's strength, divested now of hood
And winy cloak, his progress stayed—with force
The young man's hand impelled the elder to
A waiting stance, while Nephi to him spake:
    "Zoram, well you know now my disguise;
Yet not from human guile dared I so
To bear the voice and raiment of one dead—
Yes, you are masterless, unless you choose
To bear the Name of one true, living Lord,
And as your Master love the Lord of Earths—
Nay, of myself I do not speak, but through
The Spirit of High *Elohim*, who me

Directed in a bloody deed. Behold,
Within your grasp the Words of God are held,
Blood-lines of Israel, true Prophecies
That hold salvation for all humankind..
These we require—and you, if you decide
To join your strength with us, for we are led
By one who holds communion with our Lord,.
And by my name I covenant with you:
As truly lives the Lord of Israel,
As truly as my Father's Visions spoke,
As truly lives this son of Lehi's age,
As truly now I make this vow with you,
That if you join us in our wanderings,
Tread with us our God-inspired paths,
You shall a free man dwell and joy with us,
You and yours, your line conjoined with ours."
    This Zoram heard, and in his inmost heart
A note was struck, a dulcet tone, as once
From *Orpheus'* Lyre the fell beasts solemn-stilled;
And Zoram felt the approbation of
His Lord, confirmation to his soul
Of Nephi's words; and Zoram straight obeyed
The impulse from the Holy One outpoured.
Wordlessly he signaled his assent,
And shouldered once again massed Brazen Plates,
Low bowed before the might of Nephi's youth
In token of submission to the son,
Wise Lehi's last-born son, whose pledge of troth
By Zoram as a covenant was held;
And ere one hour died into the night,
With Nephi, Sam, Laman, Lemuel,
Unto the tents of Lehi, Zoram marched,
His heart of freezing fear now destitute,
His limbs and spirit warmed in friendship's glow;
For Zoram—masterless no more, but now
Possessing and possessed of One with Light—

Placed mortal cares in Nephi's competence,
And in the desert wastes he found his Lord.

BOOK XI

At Evening, Nephi again ascends the Mount of Prayer, kneeling beside an Altar; The Youth is visited by the Spirit of the Lord, who raises him to a high Mountain and offers him a Vision of his Line until the Time of Christ.

Lo, in the West, a burning orb descends,
Day's flaming Chariot, so near the Seat
Of God's sin-blinding, high Immensity,
Wheels on, while Earth is veiled in sleep;
Scarlet flames diffuse through dying Day,
Gilding crispéd autumn foliage
With bloody glow and stark intensities;
Vague whisps of feather-clouds glide tinged with *Or*
And gleam as Precious Bane across wide skies,
Across oft-changing hues of Heaven's vault;
Lo, often in such dim half-lights of Dusk
The Ancients' musings turned toward Earth's End,
Bards invoked their pagan Muses' Breaths,
Or whispered of feared *Götterdämmerung,*
Of *Ragnarok,* Twilight of the Gods,
Dim Twilight of those pagan Northern Gods
Ruling under Satan's sovereignty
As he in flight precipitous erewhile
Into the North his hosts rebellious led,
There to mold in Darkness secret thoughts

Of Mankind's overthrow and Heaven's Fall,
That he thus wrongs imaginéd avenge
Upon him by high Deity performed—
And those fell angels arméd in his crew
As pagan gods insinuate into
Coiled rolls of human history incrept;
Yet Mankind knew that *Woden*'s powers should fail,
When once the final battle hotly joined
Both dread and fey Antagonists destroys,
The Giants and the Gods; when falls the Tree
Ygdrasil, World-Ash, its roots consumed
By ruinous decay; when *Fenris-Wolf*
His banded chains shall break, and from the Sea
The *Midgard Serpent* rise to afflict the Earth
With vip'rous, burning breath; and all that was
No more continues in its former state;
Frail Earth into the Ocean-maw subsides,
Slowly sinks into a watery Death—
All is silent in the Universe
Until the highest generative Power
An Orb renewed and Earth for men and gods
In peace to share conceives and executes,
A Sphere in which vile rancor and deceit
No ingress—nay—nor entrance shall attain.
    So also, beneath hushed, quiet breath of Dusk,
Outsent as living Fire across wide vistas,
Hillocks silhouetted against blind East
Now deep'ning to its nightly cloak of black,
One mortal mind pondered Mankind's Fate
As he, with meditative step, approached
A stony Altar high atop a crested
Mountain eminence—a place secluded,
Bathed erewhile in Dawning's lustrous tears,
Smooth pearly Dews by Morning's goddess wept
To flow upon cold *Memnon*'s dark-raised Tomb,
To drench the cinerary bier of him
Who from the loins of aged *Tithonus* sprang,

Yet fated was to die beneath the sword
Of *Thetis'* wrathful son, to fall beneath
Upreared walls of *Priam*'s Citadel;
Now, ere yet *Diana* chaste arose
To gaze upon the beauteous innocence
Of slumber-wrapped *Endymion*, white stones
That signified the Altar of that God
To whom alone Mankind obeisance owes
Pulsed sanguine in the dying, passing Light
As one approached for Evening orisons;
Nephi came, with eyes downcast and heart,
To place upon the Altar of his God
Great cared and high desires within his soul.
As an agéd man he seemed, whom life
Had bent and slowed; nor glanced the valiant one
Upon bright, glorious embers of dead day,
But quickly knelt upon fast-cooling Earth
And bowed his face unto the darkened East,
From whence the Sun should surely rise in Light.
As Nephi there low-knelt, myriad points
Of fire far-strewn upon the canopy
Of Night by God's high will flamed forth,
Until those stones their crimson light subdued
And cast a star-lit silver to the sky.
Thus long did Nephi strive to break night's calm
And bend to sleepy Earth the High God's Eye,
That he in spirit and in flesh the Voice
Of God's *Creator* might perceive, that he
Long-promised visions might from Him receive.
    And in the silent dark of Eventide,
Jehovah's Voice as a might wind
Filled the waiting ears of Lehi's son;
He through whom high *Elohim* proceeds,
Who formed and shaped the emerald globe of Earth
And sent it whirling through Deep Space—yea, He
Who is the *King of Kings* and *Lord of Lords*
Spake unto a beardless youth's pure faith:

"My son, behold, 'tis I, thy God, who speaks;
Jehovah Am I Named amid bright Courts
Of Highest *Elohim*; *Jehovah* Am
I known among the seed of *Adam's* Loins;
Yet is it my Anointed Destiny,
Decreed before this Earth's foundations bore
Impress of their Creator's power, that I
Shall soon another Name possess, and too
Another form, to minister to men
And worlds in fleshly tabernacle frail.
For I am slain before all worlds were;
To satisfy with Mercy Justice cruel
Was I ordained to dwell as man with men;
Nor is that Time far hence. Yet shall thine eyes
Long slumber—and thy sons'—ere I shall come;
But in thy works, thy faith, am I well pleased."
    And as these bless<u>é</u>d words had filled his mind,
Bringing with them into him a Peace
Beyond all words, behold, bold Nephi saw,
Perceived beneath the lowering husk of Night,
A Light well up from deep within the Stones
By which he humbly knelt; a Light sublime,
That burned without consuming mortal flesh,
Yet kindled in insensate hearts of stones,
And growing, spread its burning majesty
Until it touched and entered Nephi's breast,
The seat where sage-conceal<u>é</u>d was the Spark
Which to his mortal dust gave Spirit-Life;
The Spark of Fire Celestial, that flared
In near propinquity to Heaven's Breath,
Inspired with transparency his flesh
And quick consumed impurities of soul
In him who nearby bowed his youthful head;
And from the deepest fastnesses of Sky,
As a blazing Star in Earthward path
Might glide in majesty and glorious Fire
Unto Earth's dark-veiled emerald Globe, and by

Its glow transcendent illuminate the skies
And distant, shadowed reaches of dark soil,
A second Light upon the Altar fell,
Magnifying the internal flames
Resident in Nephi's eager breast,
Until mortality could not contain
The Glory of a Presence hovering there;
For in that Earthbound Star a Form appeared,
A Form in substance man-like, in essence
Purest Spirit-Flesh refined; and thus
Evinced the *Spirit of the Lord* to him
Who highest guidance and communion sought.—
Just so, in centuries long past, had one
In righteousness Jehovah sought, had prayed
For intervention from Eternal Realms—
Jared's brother, he who led his folk
Out from Babel's massive hulking Tower,
From that Hideous Strength of red-bricked thrust
High-piled as if to mount the heights of Heaven,
At that time when mighty *Elohim*
In wrath Celestial imposed just fate
In foolish ones who would forestall their God,
Who would a Temple build to *Kolob*'s Gates,
Lest their Lord again in anger flood
Green Earth and all Mankind baptize in death;
And in his righteous ire, Heaven's Holy One
All tongues of men confused, and o'er wide Earth
Lone sons of Adam scattered, that no more
They should attempt to invade immortal heights;
Then came *Mahonri-Moriancumer*,
A large and mighty man before the lord,
To plead for favor in His sight, that they
Who shared his name and house should not be lost
And separate, but power retain to speak
And understand each other's precious words;
To this his Lord in Mercy acquiesced,
And Jared's brother fled to unpeopled plains,

Plains drought-swept and moiled by drying winds,
Bearing with him beasts of burden, seeds,
Swarms of *Deseret* (wild honey-bees,
Interminable hordes of burring winds
As numerous as sons of men who toiled
To raise the walls of *Dido*'s hermitage)
And priceless treasure—human souls that sought
To know, obey, and love *Jehovah*'s Will.
Four years into this Wilderness they trekked,
Four years unguided by Divine decree
Until again their Lord revealed His Mind;
And Jared's folk great barges built, that they
Deep, boundless Oceans cross in search of Lands
Unto them Promiséd; yet failed them Light,
Illumination for their tight-closed ships;
And thus went Jared's brother to a Mount,
Bearing with him sixteen molten stones,
That God should touch them with His Fingertips
And they should give forth constant, guiding Light.
Thus prayed *Mahonri-Moriancumer*,
With faith abiding, all-surpassing faith,
Faith that rent the veil 'twixt Heavens and Earth—
For as *Adonai* reached His mighty Hand
To summon Light within translucent stones,
Jared's brother's eyes perceived His God;
Jehovah, who as *Christ*, into this world
Should come to summon Light in human souls;
And through His act of saving Grace on Earth
Painfully effect salvation's joys
For all mortality—all sons of God
And daughters pure inhabiting far Spheres
Of life within God's Word's Hegemony,
Spirit Children placed in fleshly form
On worlds unnumbered but to His own Mind;
Yea, Earth's Creator shed His shroud of mists
His shroud of mists impenetrably bright,
To stand before man's living eyes of flesh,

Surrounded by blinding aureate glows,
Outpourings of His Spirit, which is Light;
The Stones were touched, and Jared's Folk enjoyed
Enlightenment and knowledge high bestowed.
   So also in the Latter Days a youth
In rank confusion sought immortal Guide—
Joseph, tossed upon sea-swells of lies,
Of men's philosophies, of craven gods,
Found sanctuary in a Sacred Grove,
Low-knelt beneath an arching, living vault
Of Springtime's verdant growth, and there
Unto his searching soul appeared at first
The baleful Powers of Darkness, o'ercoming,
Near o'erwhelming the unwaxen youth
Who, all his meager strength exerting full,
Burst foul fetters of Earth's Evil One.
Then suddenly he saw a Tower of Light,
Pillar-like and pure, pulsing Light
Downsent from kingly realms Celestial,
And peering through the whisp'ring foliage
Toward the growing Light that all infused
Until Day's blazing noon-bright Solar disk
As Darkness burned, as if the *Sacred Grove*
Were a vortex in heliocentric Space;
For midst life-burgeoning trunks and sporting shoots,
The Son of Sons and Light of Ruling Light,
In concert with the Omnipotent Father-God,
Appeared, and spake good news of full rebirth,
Of restitution of all things once lost,
Of invocation to the Final Days.
   So now, as Nephi knelt before white stones,
High-altared stones suffused with silky Light,
Before him stood the *Spirit of the Lord*,
White of countenance as sun-drenched snows,
Robed in flowing gown of purity;
With Voice magistral spake the Shining One,
Inclined his words to Nephi's eager soul:

"Nephi, son of Lehi, Prophet of
The wanderings of Joseph's wayward Seed,
Those branches that grow o'er the Fountain's Walls
Until establishéd in Earth's most fertile
Places; Nephi, hearken to my words:
Behold, in thee and in thy Faith am I
Well pleased, I and all who look to Earth
From realms Celestial, participants
In Councils of the Gods Divine. Behold,
Full hast thou thy anointment high fulfilled
And art prepared—a Prophet to thy God."
    And now, behold, as Nephi heard these words
His spirit soared above the blighted plains
On which his father's tents of rough-cured skins
Bore mute evidence of reaching heights
From which young Nephi's eyes now downward searched;
Yea, as flocked, feathered lords of air he rose
In rapid flight, was caught away unto
A mountainous eminence, exceeding high,
The which before had never known man's tread;
And from this height, as *Moses* on God's Mount,
As *Adam* on the Mount of Revelation,
Could Nephi see *his* Promised Land—nay,
Not dry, strict confines of Judah's bounds,
Or Israel's, nor yet alone the vast
Unpeopled continents toward the West,
Washed by peaceful suns and gentle seas,
Washed by gentle suns and peaceful seas,
Within its heart of hearts True *Paradise*,
Near *Adam-ondi-Ahman,* place of Prayer
And blesséd Convocation graced by him,
Our noble Sire, the Ancient One of Days,
Who yet must come to give accounting of
His Stewardship o'er all the Sons of Men;
No, Nephi bold behold this Earth's green Globe,
The Earth reserved for highest soul-delight,
That must through flame and purifying fire,

Through Heaven's seering Heat unleashéd pass,
That she might thus become a Promised Realm,
Pure Kingdom of Celestial Ones redeemed;
Yea, for a moment's space saw Nephi all,
His mind perceived this Sphere's immensity,
And he its people through all mortal time;
Then spake again the *Spirit of the Lord*:
   "My son, look now upon thine own." And lo,
Across his eyes a veil was partly drawn,
And vast expanses blotted out, great folks
No more paraded in his sight; instead,
A narrow segment of the Earth remained,
A segment undiscovered to the East
Until revealed, discovered through the Hand
Of Him who such Lands gave unto His own.
The Voice continued low: "Behold thy line;
Behold the consequences of thy Act,
Of thy obedience high in slaying him
Who stood between thy People and their Past,
Their History recorded on Brass Plates;
For difficult and hard the task you seemed,
To shed a fellow-human's life-red blood—
Yet was it necessary, that all men
Of Lehi's lineage my Truths behold.
And now, my son, look well upon thy Seed;
For thou shalt see its History from hence
Until I come; and what thou seest, indite,
Record upon the engraved Plates of Brass,
Those scenes that in thy memory remain
When this, thy Vision, draws unto its close;
Many things thou shalt this day perceive,
Happenings yet centuries removed
From thee and thine—such shalt thou not reveal,
But fast entrenched within thy soul retain;
Nephi, son of highest *Elohim*,
Brother to the *Savior* yet to come,
To *Christ,* the *One Anointed* for all Time

To save the sinful sons of heaven's King:
Nephi, look upon futurity!"
    At this express command bold Nephi turned,
Removed his transformed eyes from Spirit-form,
And gazed upon the wheeling Earth. And lo,
The first great Vision met his wond'ring sight:
Lehi's train, augments by the host
Of *Ishmael*'s family—Ishmael, of
The line of *Joseph*'s heir, whose daughters young
Were fair and beauteous; and one there was
Of spirit gentle, sweet, of faith intense,
At whose approaching smile young Nephi's heart
In quick abandon surged and burned within,
A kindred spirit he her felt, by him
Erst known before this Earth's created Birth.
And as he gazed upon her matchless form,
As he an unknown stirring in his loins
Perceived and vainly strove to quell, to calm,
The *Spirit of the Lord* thus softly spake:
"Thy wife and mother of thy unborn Line;
She whose spirit known and loved by thee
Has been preserved by mine own hand for thee,
And thou preserved by mine own hand for her,
That ye might wed and in the Promised Land
full blessings high enjoy in thy Posterity;
Yet shall this Vision fade, that ye might grow
In love, unknowing of this foreordained
Decree, but rather learning slow through life
Of two choice souls one greater Soul to forge."
    And as the Spirit spake, behold, the scene
Was subtly changed; again the desert wastes,
But now with swelling hints of verdant heights
And gleaming, living seas of Heaven's hue.
In Nephi's mind the setting cleared away, gray mists
Obscuring sight, were burned away, and he
In great astonishment himself beheld,
Upon green shores of *Irreantum* vast,

Of *Many Waters,* through dread wilderness
By God's own Will directed, by the Globe
Of Gold, the *Liahona*'s artistry,
That *Compass* which through Faith alone would point
True paths toward great Lehi's destiny,
And which through Nephi's power should never fail,
Which yet must come to Lehi's reaching hand
Short time before the death of Ishmael
And rude rebellion raised by Laman's voice—
Rebellion raised by wild foment of pride,
Quelled as One Great Voice chastised the man
And those who hearkened to his glozening lies.
Yea, eight years passed since Laban's sacrifice
Would bring frail Lehi's troop unto the Sea,
And there the Voice of God again should sound.
And in his Vision's brightness Nephi
His elder brethren twain opposing stand,
Reviling him for his divine desires;
And Nephi bold beheld his Lord's commands,
Succeeding to himself in future years
As he again in mortal danger dwelt,
In threat of death at Laman's raging hands:
"Stretch forth thy hand unto thy brethren-flesh,
And I, thy Lord, will shock them that they know
That I, their Lord, have chosen thee mine own";
And thus it passed that Nephi's hand forth-stretched
Pure Powers of the Lord out-pulsed, and they
Who doubted Nephi's truth were shook and feared,
So much so that they dared not to speak, but knelt
And worshipped Nephi, worshipped Nephi's God.
    Yet no more of these sights saw Nephi's eyes,
For soon the flowing Visions transposed Sea
For Earth, as Lehi's family forth-sailed
In ship, by God inspired, for Promised Lands,
And Nephi's soul was wrung with burning pain
As he beheld light, mindless revelry
In Lehi's eldest and their willful wives;

For they no more gave heed unto the Power
That thither brought them, but with wildness vile
And merriment abused the God of Gods
(Merriment itself not the telling cause
Of God's deep frown, for Joy and Happiness
Are mortal rights and that deep cause for which
All Adam's progeny exists—to know
True Joy; but this that Nephi saw was false,
This merriment found source and expression
In ridiculing Sacred Things, making
Light of that deserving honor's dignity),
Yea, Lehi's eldest two abused their God,
And Nephi saw sore pain in Lehi's soul,
Hoar Lehi and Sariah near to death—
And righteousness with cruelty confined,
For Laman and Lemuel overcame
All force of argument by Lehi, Sam,
Opposed, and Nephi tightly bound with ropes,
For Nephi rightly chose not to oppose
With Godly force inherent in his mind
And thus constrain his wayward kin to hear,
Obey, and yet not understand the Will
Of God; and Nephi tightly bound with ropes,
Felt, as his bonds were closed, yea, felt the Lord
Withdraw His guiding hand, the *Liahona*'s Orb
No more directions gave, and Lehi's ship
Lay wildly tossed upon frothed, billowing Seas,
Until in fear and mortal frightedness
In face of watery Tomb and imminence
Of dire Judgments through the Ocean's might,
Laman and crass Lemuel perceived
That God's commandments counter to them ran;
They loosened Nephi's bonds and him revived,
Into his hands the *Liahona* thrust
And with apparent penitence desired
Their younger brother's prayers on their behalf.
He knew the truth, yet granted them the hope

Of true repentance, and forgave, and stood.
And thus it came to pass that as he stood
And took the Compass-Globe, all tumult died,
Harsh winds diminishéd, and Lehi's sons
Soon touched the shores of Lands long Promiséd.
    This Nephi saw, the while the Spirit spake
Soft words of comfort and of warning fears;
Yet greater wounds in store pierced Nephi's soul,
As in the Promised Land the elder two
Again fell prey to Satan's powerful wiles
And threatened death to Nephi's righteousness;
Until—with ancient Lehi's deathly sleep
And respite from all sorrows of the Earth—
Rebellion rose, and internecine strife;
The Stem of Joseph's branch divided then
Into two lines opposed: the *Red*, whose minds
Engrossed were with murderous thoughts and will,
With hopes of bloody vengeance through long years,
As Laman's progeny their white-hot hate
And mortal fear of Nephi's righteous seed—
Yea, and their fear of Nephi's written words
Whose witness bold against the *Lamanites*
Should ever stand, indicting wickedness
And vile deceit when those of Laman's blood
Should *choose* to practice evil ways and live
In conscious sin, should urge transgression of
The panoply of Laws Divine for men,
Beginning with cruel Laman's twisted ploy
To bring about the deaths of Nephi, Sam,
And gentle wives and children of those two
Who firm believed their Revelation's words,
That Nephi as the *Prophet-Priest* should rule;
And in their lair-like, wilderness retreats,
Laman's dark-minded sons degenerate,
No more a Chosen Folk unto the Lord,
Increased in numbers and in willfulness,
Their copper nakedness ill-clothed in skins,

Their burnished flesh adorned with earth-delved tints—
Bloody scarlet, ashen white, and black
As deep and secret as the murky night—
That thus more fearful they in war appeared;
And to these Red opposed should stand the *White*,
Sons of Nephi, bright of flesh and soul,
And heirs to choicest blessings in the Land,
Contingent upon obedience to Law;
A bright and a delightsome Folk, well-versed
In all civility, in music's arts,
And poetry, whose only hopes in life
Were for eternal peace and brotherhood.
    Thus Nephi saw division in his race.
And in his deepest anguish called he forth
Unto the Spirit of the Lord, and framed
Soul-wrenching fears that shook his young-man's heart:
"How long, O Holy One, shall this prevail,
That scions of a single Line shall war,
Unrighteousness with righteousness opposed,
Brothers, marked as with Sign from God
Of their unworthiness, against the sons
Of their own Father warring with intent
To murder, pillage, from this Earth destroy?"
    Then spake the Paraclete, with gentle calm:
"Behold, my son, ere many years shall pass,
The line dividing White from Dark shall blur
As righteousness declines and evil grows;
For that which here appears a darkened flesh
Is but a shadow of a darkened soul,
Set upon thy brothers' progeny
In token of their fathers' erring ways—
For Laman, Lemuel, and sons of him
Who with thy father joined, Ishmael,
Shall split asunder from the Trunk of Truth;
Yet as the Bright Ones—*Nephites*—firm obey,
Their God shall prosper them upon this Land,
They shall accrue great riches and shall rule,

And joys and miracles untold be theirs;
Yet as they fail to hold high Covenants
Once made with Israel's Living Holy One
(And that they shall fail I know, yet knowing
Do not cause but more deeply grieve their choice),
They shall decay and fall as rotting fruit
From healthy vines; and cease to be a Folk
Delightsome, light, and pleasing to their God;
And blessings erst them promised shall devolve
Upon the righteous of the remnant Seed,
Who in the course of centuries shall learn
And shall accept the Truths that *Christ* shall bring.
And now, my son, behold the history
Of those to whom obedience means naught."
    Nephi turned, and as he looked he wept;
Few instances of Light did he perceive:
An ancient King, with hoary hair and white,
Speaking from a Temple's shadowed cool,
Praising men who in this life were gods—
Or as the gods—who served their fellowmen
As men would serve their God; a Patriarch,
Abinadi, the Voice of God, bound
Amid red flesh-consuming flames of Fire,
Condemned by one unworthy of a Throne
And *Noah*'s ancient Name, yet in his pain
And mortal torments' gnawing agonies
Abinadi with patience, fortitude,
Withstood the flames, repeating prophecies
Revering Christ who was to come to Earth,
Bearing witness to the Spirit's Truth;
Four royal sons, and one—a Prophet's heir—
Who erewhile fought against their Lord's desires
Until converted by Celestial Sights
And Sounds, then going with true Priesthood's Call,
With Priesthood's awesome Powers, to bear the Word
Unto their mortal enemies, to bring
Soul-light unto deep-darkened Ones;

And yet again a military form,
Unbowed by armor's weight and fearful toil
Defending home and family from them
Who in their murky ignorance would that
Destroy wherein for all Salvation lay,
He, bearing high the *Title of Liberty,*
The painted Words: "*In Memory of our God,
Of our Religion, Freedom, and our Peace;
Our Wives and Children dear!*"—inspiring call
To rightwiseness, waving high above
A fallen and degraded polity,
Resulting in conversion of erring hearts
Unto straight paths ordained before the Worlds.
    These Nephi saw, and for those instants Joy
Flooded through his heart, that righteousness thus
Stood before sin; yet more than these of ill,
Of Evil's sway upon a blighted land
Immersed in Immorality and Sin;
For as the White-graced Ones apostatized,
The Hand of God protective might withdrew—
And years would pass in blood and death and tears,
Long years stained as if by bloody ragged
Pinions on a soaring wing diseased,
Until at last prophetic words bore flight
And once again high obedience renewed
Brought life and hope and Light unto green Lands.
    Thus Nephi saw, and as he saw he wept
For Lehi's progeny who yet would fall
Into the Abyss of unrepentant sin,
Convinced by *Mephisthelean* wiles
That all in *Zion* prospered...until they fell,
Convicted by their free-willed acts performed,
And gently led until enchained to Hell.
    Then Nephi's visionary orbs were turned
Again away from dark Futurity
Unto white, shining garments of the One
Before him standing on wind-cloven Air

With feet secure as if upon golden
Breastworks on a gleaming Altar bared;
Horror in his twisted visage formed
(In spite of Heavenly Visions seen)
As he upon the Mentor-Spirit gazed,
At thought of rampant wickedness and fall
Revealed through Heaven's visionary powers—
For Nephi *Evil* Incarnate had seen,
As if, with *Gloriana*'s Holy Knight,
He had experienced that vile Parade
Of proud *Lucifera* (as men her called),
Who first before the Redcross Knight appeared,
High-seated on a golden, jeweled Throne
Within heart-depths concealed of Pride's vain House;
The beauteous *Lucifera* adorned
With *Phaeton*'s fiery graces, served by six—
This brash usurper, progeny of Hell
Who from her Throne descending chose her seat
Within a gilded Chariot, slow-drawn
By beasts unequal, suited to the *Crew*
Of servile Councilors to Goddess Pride:
Idleness, upon a slothful Ass,
Sluggish and somnambulant, nigh drowned
In waves of worldly, woeful weariness,
Who from his drugged sleep roused would stare
With empty thoughts and rheumy eyes, unsure
Of stance, his leaden soul depressed by sloth;
His mind a vacuum of stup'rous thoughts confused;
Next *Gluttony*, upon his filthy Swine,
Immoderate Unwisdom uncreate,
His hideous, bloated shape with luxury swelled
His mind diseased by riot and excess,
Ever fearful, lest dire Want should come
And him reduce unto a healthy trim,
Yet never knowing fully essential
Differences that lie between true Want
And false, beguiling, convincing Desire,

Who failed to find the Moderate in all;
Then *Lechery,* amount Sin's bearded Goat,
Who symbolized the basest lusts of all,
The Procreative Powers abused, debased,
Perverted to a raging heat unruled,
A lewdness tainting loins with foul disease,
Desiring irresponsibility
And glut of passion without progeny;
And by these greedy *Avarice* close heeled,
Avarice upon a laden Beast,
The hump-backed desert Beast, wretched Greed,
Who feels unending Need, is tortured by
Unending Covetise, never pleased,
Never satisfied by the measure he
Possesses but seeks all ways to rule his
Unsuspecting neighbors' wealth as his own;
The fifth approached, malicious *Envy*'s corse,
Upon a Wolf securely mounted, clad
In robes with ornamented Eyes thereon,
Wherewith he all could see—and all desire—
And in his secret bosom harbored coiled
A Serpent—base desire for other's Weal—
For never could he see another's wealth
In gold, or family, or happiness,
But inwardly his bowels churned and writhed;
Close behind, revenging *Wrath* drew near,
Upon a Lion, brandishing a flame,
With eyes that glowed as livid scarlet fire,
Yet flesh as deadly gray as cooling ash
Within the fire pit at Morn when still
Cool darkness lingers on and yet no eye
Of gleaming coal looks forth—stained with blood
His cloak, with blood of Innocents deprived
By him of life and high felicity,
For he no fleshly appetites controlled,
But struck and maimed and killed as pleasure bid,
Most dangerous in self-confusing guise

Of rabid righteousness or holy ire,
Counterfeiting Acts without true Holiness;
Behind these six, with *Pride,* their chiefest good,
Stiff-necked, unbending in blind Arrogance,
Swelled with his Peculiarity, yet
Ravening to seem as one with mindless
Hordes, all the while convinced of his degree,
Vaunting his sly superiority—
Behind these seven clad in uniforms
Ever-changing, ever-shifting and thus
Forever new and pleasing-seeming to
Struggling hearts and minds too often gullible,
Strode raging *Sathan,* leathern whip in hand,
And ever as *Lucifera*'s compeers
Their forward impetus decreased, he lashed
Her lazy team again to violence.
    So seemed unto the sage and solemn Bard
Hell's *Seven Sins*; so drew *Eliza*'s Singer
Portraits of these hideous Deadly Ones;
Yet Nephi, in his Vision's scope, beheld
Their more than hideous Reality,
As *Pride* burst forth among his white-skinned Folk—
Infernal Pride of place, of wealth, of blood,
Vaunting above all merit earned by toil
And humble obedience to God's Laws,
Perverting all true love, fraternal hope—
Soon followed by disgracéd *Indolence,*
Carnal appetites, *Greed,* and sting
Of *Envy*'s serpent-fangs, until in *Wrath*
Each man against his Brother raised dread Ire,
And Lehi's Seed engulféd was in Death,
Self-consumed before the *Throne* of *Pride.*
    This Nephi saw; he wept, yet as he knelt
The Voice once more flowed out upon cool Air,
His Messenger Celestial thus spake:
"My son, look well upon thy People's Sins,
And grieve that Wickedness such might should wield.

Yet all is not perverse and desolate;
Some few remain obedient to my Law.
Behold, my son, the Consequences of
Obedience to God's ordained Decrees."

BOOK XII

Nephi's Vision continues, as Nephi witnesses the Signs accompanying the Birth of Christ in the Old World; The Prophecies of destruction on the American Continent coincidental with The Crucifixion are shown to be fulfilled; Nephi seeks to participate in the Coming of Christ to the Inhabitants of the Americas, but is restrained by the Spirit.

THE *Spirit of the Lord* to Nephi spake;
Nephi looked, and soon beheld a man,
A noble, dusk-toned man, with flashing eyes
And coppered flesh beneath his raven hair
(And by such outward signs knew Nephi well
That here was one who shared rash Laman's blood,
That here was one who shared rash Laman's curse
Of darkened flesh to signify his sin—
Laman's sin—of willfulness against God).
Long sat he still, this seeming-man of flesh,
Through Nephi's visionary eyes revealed,
Long sat he still, intent upon a text
Before him held, with eager mien and heart
Consuming words by Prophets' hands inscribed.
    "Nephi," spake the Messenger, "observe,
And know that thus the History of Thy Seed,
With Knowledge drawn from Laban's Plates conjoined,
Knowledge of the Lineage high and past

Mistakes of *Eber*'s erring sons revealed
Through Prophecies and vatic Visions shared,
Has here succeeded to thine enemies—
Enemies alone in their unwise
Conceit, through fathers' lines descending strong,
Of Nephite treachery and base deceit
Practiced on their unsuspecting Sire,
Great Lehi's eldest (and unworthy) son—
Enemies no more through their belief
And faith in Him who shall be born to Earth;
This grandson many times removed from him
Who sought thy life to crush—this Lamanite—
Shall preach Salvation to closed, sin-stopped ears
Of Nephite sons; and they who apprehend
His Truths—which Truths from Laban's Plates descend
In one unbroken Line through thine own Plates,
Thy Father's Plates, each a record sealed
By Truth, preserved for future heirs of Truth—
Yea, all to come who apprehend his Truths
Shall know and taste the bliss of Heaven's Tree."
    And as the Voice spake on, the Vision changed;
No more did Nephi's eyes behold the Man
In silent thought and meditation's peace,
No more did Nephi see great *Samuel*
At rest among the hearths of Laman's seed
To study from the righteous Words of God,
Withdrawn, contemplative, eager to Know;
Nay, now he stood atop a city's wall,
A massive wall of blood-red masonry,
Encrimsoned by Earth's sun's expiring rays,
Upon his head a dusky Crown of Fire
(It seemed) and draping him a Cloak of Skins
To hide his sanguine nakedness from eyes
Long grown unmindful of true modesty,
Who in their grossly garbed Desires portrayed
A deeper Nakedness of soul and heart.
His voice roared forth to speak of future things,

Of wondrous things within five years to come—
And many, hearing, fell upon their knees
In humble token of repentant hearts.
He spake of Light—a Day, a Night, a Day—
That should be as one Day, as if no Night
Had settled down upon recumbent Earth,
As if the Sun had ceased his nightly rest
To rush his flaming Chariot 'mid bright stars
And all the Universe from sleep awake,
And all the Universe awake from sleep;
He spake of one great *Star* that should be seen
In token of the descent of God's own Son;
He spake of further signs of Darkness, Death,
When in the Eastern spheres God's Son must die.
Then with a cry the Lamanite down-leapt
And disappeared into his native land
Ere messengers outsent their flinty tips,
Him pierced, and loosed the spirit of his flesh,
Ere arrows swift and vip'rous him afflict
With poisonous breath and fangs blood-red and sharp
And him impel into Eternities;
Yea, *Samuel* dissolved from Nephi's Vision's
Frame, no more to be heard nor seen among
Base Nephites in broad Zarahemla's land.
   This Nephi wondering beheld; yet soon
His Vision once again transformed appeared,
And Nephi saw a sport of his own branch
In deep despair beneath a Doom of Death;
For Wickedness held sovereign sway among
All peoples in pale Nephite's nation's bounds,
And subsequent cruel Death decreed for them
Who credence placed in Samuel's Prophecies
Thrown from the walls of Zarahemla's might
(Mighty Citadel, now grown through false choice
Into a *Pandemonium* to infect
The fertile Promised Land with evil's blight),
Thrown in face of rampant vileness;

Yet some believed—a prophet *Nephi* named
In token of his parents' hopes that he
Might grow in stature mighty, and in faith,
Descendant from true loins of Nephite Kings,
In prayer sincere, suppliant, sought his God,
Him to entreat for Mercy's sustenance
And justice paid unto God's faithful ones.
And Lehi's son beheld this man in prayer,
His namesake kneeling on sand-scoured shores
As *Oceanus'* waves caressed dry Land
And fiery *Sol* descended into Night.
Long had he knelt in feeling prayer, this son
Of Nephi's posterity, long craved surcease
From deep uncertainty through Light revealed;
And Lehi's son beheld the consequence
Of righteous faith implicitly applied—
For as the kneeling *Sun* impinged upon
Far waves dyed true cerulean by depth,
And with fire's tender touch a blush called forth
Throughout blue Heavens up to the Virgin *Moon*,
Behold, bright *Day* diminished not in might,
Nor *Darkness* spread his soporific cowl
In one slow, symphonic harmony
Upon the face of yet-unsleeping *Earth*;
And through cool, lightened, freshened, living *Air*
Breathed out a Voice triumphant, gentle, hushed;
And he upon jeweled shores looked up in Joy,
As if his heart's desires accomplished were,
As if his heart infuséd were with Joy
And that for which he hoped had come to pass.
The Voice breathed hushed, and thus the Message spake:
"My Son, I see thy Faith, and I rejoice.
Because of thy abounding Confidence
In me, and in my Words engraved upon
Cold Metal Plates of Prophecies preserved
Through generations—from thy Fathers' flight
Into waste Wilderness unto this Day—

Because of thy unfailing faith I speak:
Behold, I am *Jesus Christ*, thy Lord,
The *One* foretold from Time's beginning Day—
This Night I come unto near Eastern spheres,
This Night shall I, as Child, in flesh descend
And in the Morning be as Man on Earth;
As proof thereof, behold my Sign!—*Christ's Star*!"
     Sounds as echoes died into *Night*'s still;
And as the golden disk of Nature's Eye,
The lidless Eye unfailing, regal gold,
Slow-slipped behind blue Water's curvature
A flickering Light appeared in Eastern skies,
Diminished, flamed—then pulsed in glowing Might,
Steadily increasing in its Might,
Until its brilliance seared the mortal Globe
And one great Star encompassed all in Light.
     And then it seemed that all was muted, soft,
As far away, within a stable warm,
A Maiden sat, with Infant-Babe in arms,
Wordless Infant, Word of God's abiding
Love for daughters, sons encased in flesh;
And in awed Nephi's ears a melody
As if of Choirs Seraphic lingered long,
Fading, yes, but echoing through his heart
(As it would echo long through all the Earth,
Resounding in the Songs of Christmas-Tide
Outbreathed by Children's Voices to the night,
Voices joined unto the Angel Choir
In homage-odes sung to the Greatest Child's
Nativity)—Echoing through his heart
To join with Nephi's own impelling song,
Song of Praise, yet muted Lullaby.
     At this his Mentor's Voice uprose subdued
To interpret for the mortal's fragile sense
Significance of that by him previewed:
"Thy heart is filled with passing, bursting Joy
As that thou seest, the Advent of Earth's God,

The Coming of the Christ to save all Worlds.
And justly so, for at His spoken Word
All *Cosmos* organized from elements
Preëxistent yet unformed in present
State, awaiting only Voice Supreme
And high Authority to join as form,
To organize as planets, moons, and stars;
And at His Spoken Word did Man arise,
Adam-Father and Mother-*Eve* arise,
Shake off insensate dust, and claim their realm,
Intelligences co-Eternal, now
Progressed to stature proximate to Gods;
Thus at His Condescension toward all
Should all created Life bow down its head
In meekest praise and high humility.
Thus should it be, yet shall it not be so!
Look now upon thy Promised Soil!"
    And Nephi looked, beheld the *Infant* Faith
Among all Nephite followers of Christ;
Beheld incipient divisiveness
As some held forth against Mosaic Law,
Contending that Christ's mortal Birth destroyed
Necessity for firm obedience
To Words decreed upon steep *Sinai*'s heights.
Yet was this not fell source of deepest fear,
But rather inroads vicious, cruel, made
By secret, dark, and evil robber bands
Erst formed through *Gadianton*'s guileful wiles
(Beneath the Ægis of *Apollyon,*
Dread Lord of Realms *Chthonic*, he who fell
From true Celestial Courts, by his misdeeds
And high o'erweening vaunting ostracized,
Who now himself contented in soul-death
For Adam's children, sin-bound and debased).
Thus through Infernal Counsel robbers formed,
And high begirt within lush, emerald Mounts,
They raised a massive, stone-bound Citadel

Of stones close-fit, without a narrow seam,
Unconquerable, invisible to those
Who knew not secret words and hidden ways;
And to this fastness streamed men discontent,
Outcasts, murderers, and fleeing thieves,
Both Lamanite and Nephite blood corrupt
Concentrated 'mid Andean heights.
    As Nephi watched, long years sped quickly by,
First ten, they twenty since the *Holy Birth*;
Greensward encroached upon once-furrowed fields,
Well-traveled roadways through disuse decayed,
Treasures hidden in the bowels of earth
Evaporated with the rising dews,
And nothing sure of virtue or of value
Fast remained within its owner's grasp;
For Secret Combinations had increased
As their corrosive Power consumed all Peace,
And deeds in darkest Secret done replaced
The Light of Sacred things performed in Light;
Nations polarized—the righteous fled
Unto their walléd homes, nor dared they sow
Lest Gadianton's callous thieves should reap
With reaping more of rapine than of joy;
While wicked men against men righteous warred,
The Land of Lehi's high inheritance
Lay torn (not for the last time, Nephi feared,
Nor the first, but worst for following so
Closely on that Night of universal
Harmony)—lay torn, bespattered, befouled
With shed and innocent-spilled brethren-blood.
    And as the Time drew near when *Christ* should die—
Thirty years and three since Samuel's Sign,
The *Star,* betokened His Nativity—
Behold, dissension threatened faithful flocks,
Pollutions spread abroad through all the Land,
As if in clouds of noxious smokes exhaled,
Instilled by greed exterior and pride,

By loss of faith among professéd Saints;
Yea, so great were men's abominations
And perversities, hell-deeds rampant,
That Murder overt stained once-Promised Soil,
The *Chief Judge* slain upon his Judgment Seat,
And civil order slain throughout all folds;
Every one unto close Kindred clove,
Lest other raise in fury blood-soaked hands
And slay with fearlessness before the Law,
And slay with fearlessness despite all Law.
    This Nephi saw, and fain would turn away
Tormented eyes from scenes calamitous;
Yet turned he not, for *Horror*'s fascination
Held him bound, as did the Heavenly Voice;
And now great happenings were seen abroad;
Across the guiltless face of suffering Earth
The Promised Land withdrew in horror-fear,
Tempests, floods, and quakings o'er the Land
With fracturing force disrupted Spring-smooth soils;
Molten bowels of Earth herself spewed forth
In agony; cities vast consumed
By sulfurous flames, by whirlwinds' deadly breath,
By wild encroachment of the savage seas;
Smooth-hewn stones, close-joined to form high ways
On which trade, commerce, and civility
Depended once, severed and destroyed;
High places thrust down low with violence,
Low places elevate above green heights
Assigned according to His primal Will
Who erst composed this whirling turquoise Globe.
And though three hours in desolation passed,
All these occurred within the space of breaths
To Nephi's frighted soul, nor failed loud cries
Of dying tongues to pierce his woe-filled ears;
Yet comfort none did Lehi's son perceive
Amid destruction, cataclysm, death;
For when had ceased all perturbations of

Distresséd Earth, internal flames subsided,
Turmoiled Seas withdrew from muddied shores,
Behold, and all was calm and pacified,
Quiet with heart-stopping silences,
Then stretched from Eastward shores a Cloud of Night,
Coldly boiling Westward, until all
Beneath *Diana*'s silvery, singing Sphere
Was husked in thick, impenetrable Mist—
Mist darker than the mist of *Paradise*
That evil whispered to Eve's night-time dreams
But this no evil cloud but rather loss,
Absense of all Light, now God lay Dead.
And thus it came to pass that vaporous Black
Invested all the Land, 'til none might see,
But only feel soul-choking, blinding Damps;
None might see, who had survived the throes
And sympathetic wrenchings of pained Earth,
Who felt within her molten depths sharp pangs
For her Creator, thrust upon a Cross;
Yea, none might see, for Light was nowhere found—
Dry and splintered woods, tall waxen tapers,
Torches drenched in oils combustible—
None would flame with fires visible
Though fire perchance consumed their matter raw,
Flame and oxidation's heat consumed,
Destroyed, transformed to ash—*but with no Light*;
Nor could *Apollo*'s hidden face be seen,
Or form of Moon, or Stars, who in the hush
And solemn still funereal, constrained
And veiled their incandescent powers in shame;
For He whose Spirit is the Light of *Sun*,
Of *Moon,* of *Stars,* of *Earths* eternally,
Was gone, withdrawn into that crystal Sphere
Beyond all mortal ken; three days withdrawn,
And yet three days immured within dread dark
Of Earth-Leviathan's sepulchral Maw,
His mortal husk upon a stone-slab bier

Within a Garden near *Jerusalem*—
Innocence slain lest multitudes dwindle,
Perish, and sleep in timeless unBelief.
And in the Western Spheres had many died,
Many in darkness, though not all;
Light had failed, yet lived the Nephite folk
With righteous Lamanites conjoined in tears,
While from the Mist's benighting density
Rose forth unto the ears of Heaven's God
Great mournings, howling, weeping from men's hearts,
Groanings of survivors in their fears.
    And from one place could Nephi hear their moan:
"O, had we but repented of our sins
Before the Coming of this Day of Death;
For then our Brethren's flesh had not been burned,
Consumed in mighty Zarahemla's fall."
And from another place he heard sad words:
"O, had we but repented of our sins
Before the Coming of this Day of Doom;
O, had we not true Prophets of our Lord
Despiséd, stoned, and cast into Death's Wilds;
Then had our mothers and our daughters lived,
Then had our sons and fathers yet drawn breath,
Then had our children laughed unto blue skies
Who now lie deep-entombed within wall-graves
Of crushed Moronihah, beneath dark earth."
    This spake frail voices from Morian mists;
And Nephi wept, and raised in mourning tones
His own lamenting, tearful harmony;
Yet spake the Messenger to Lehi's son,
With Voice triumphant, Mien victorious:
"Behold, thou son of man: The wicked pass,
Unjust ones stain no longer Western Lands,
And Righteousness alone survives harsh Death;
Look now, thou son of Adam's long-lived Seed,
And see the Culmination of thy Hopes!
Witness now Salvation in the Earth,

And final meaning of all Prophecy!"
    At these exultant syllables all sounds,
All wails and lamentations silent fell,
Until a calm unbroken conquered worlds;
Then from bright depths of Heaven's hidden Soul
A Voice was heard by all in Darkness' grip,
A Voice of Power, which thus its message framed:
"Woe, woe unto weak, unrepentant ones
Who on this evanescent Globe sojourn.
Fell Satan and his cohorts fallen laugh
Because of sons and daughters slain in sin,
Who once were numbered to my *Chosen Folk*
But fell through their abominations vile.
Behold, I cause high stony blood-stained walls,
Zarahemla's haughty pride, to flame,
Consumed by Heaven's never-cooling Wrath;
The City of Moroni have I drowned,
With its inhabitants, beneath Salt Seas
Because of their perverse iniquities;
Behold, Moronihah the Great
Have I entombed beneath dense mounds of sod,
And also its inhabitants, to hide
Their wickedness—for guiltless blood of saints
And prophets by them slain, by them destroyed
With full consciousness, cries unto me;
The City of Gilgal is sunk in Earth,
And others have I burned with righteous fires,
Or baptized unto death with salty waves,
That blood of Innocents by evil slain
No more rise up to me. And now, behold,
Ye who are spared because of righteousness,
Will ye not repent and turn to me?
I Am Jesus Christ, the Son of God.
The Heavens and the Earths created I,
And all that in them dwell; I come to save
From sin the fallen child of Man and God.
I Am Jesus Christ, the Son of God.

I grieve that wickedness has fouled the Land
And drawn my people to the Gates of Death;
I weep, and with me weep the Hosts of Heaven.
   "I come, and thus fulfill the Holy Writ
That testifies of me; and ye who looked
With faith toward this Day, the same receive
My Powers within themselves to be as Gods;
And these shall offer hearts in broken pride,
With spirit contrite, and repent, and they
Through Fire and Spirit unto me baptized shall be.
   "Thus I say, whiche'er of ye shall come
In deep contrition unto me, the same
Shall I receive, from all the ends of Earth."
   Thus spake the Voice of Heaven's Omnipotence
In Nephi's Vision of Futurity,
And as it spake, the worlds in their circled
Orbs, the Stars and Galaxies that wheel in
Vast precision through distances of Space
Gave Voice in one grand, triumphant Chord,
As if the universe its Voice had found
To sing in praise its God's creative Hand,
And Myth transposed to stark Reality
With Music signaling, symbolizing
God's unbounded Love, redemptive All.
All this bold Nephi heard and saw and knew;
Yet failéd not the impetus of Sight,
For Nephi thus saw three Days pass away;
And on a Morn the Dark dispersed and fled
Beneath bright flaming might of Heaven's Son;
The firm Earth ceased to tremble and to quake
And all tumultuousness dispersed away;
Indeed, a remnant of the folk was spared,
The moiety more righteous than the rest,
More adamant in heeding principles
Whose operation mediates for Earth
Rich blessings from sweet Heaven's heights; yea, these
Of Lehi's loins who had believed were spared,

Nor sunk and buried in Earth's loam, nor drowned
Beneath black, briny froth and welling waves,
Nor burned by flaming fire, nor cruelly crushed,
Nor borne away within wild whirlwinds.
Mourning and lamenting voices ceased,
As morning swelled with joyous praise informed,
Praise unto Man's Lord, Earth's Christ, Heaven's King.
    Nephi's Mentor turned to him and spake,
Æthereal countenance subdued and mild,
Yet deep suffused with Joys inexpressible:
"Behold, the words fulfilled that Prophets spake
And faithful Scribes enchronicled on Plates
In Laban's Treasure-hoard concealed until
Brought forth through thy judicious, guiltless act,
To bring Salvation's Knowledge to thy Seed."
    And now it seemed as if all Space had changed,
And all perceptions of Degree and Form
Altered were to Nephi's o'erfilled mind;
It seemed that Nephi knelt no more upon
The Mountain-Height next Heaven's Spirit-Form;
Instead, the son of ancient Lehi stood
As if among a spacious multitude,
A Congregation vast assembléd
Before a luminescent Edifice
Of ungrained brilliance, snowy-white and bright.
In the distance, shattered Towers mute—
Gray stone, red fire-hardened brick, veined woods—
Bespoke internal powers that shook grave Earth,
And all around were signs of recent ruin;
Yet stood the Temple's parapets unharmed,
Its pillars rising as two fiery Beams
In supplication to their burning God,
As long before the Golden Ones were raised
Before high portals by *Solomon* the *Wise*,
"In Him is Strength," and "He will Establish"—twins
Of precious ore erected to the Lord,
Jachin and *Boaz* on *Zion*'s heights;

So appeared the ornamental fires
Before the Temple's glow in Bountiful;
Near high Eastern portals, golden-bronze,
Where People gathered, deep in thought and prayer,
Speaking softly of this *Jesus Christ*
Whose death-signs had convulsed and wrenched great Earth.
    And it came to pass that as the people stood,
They heard a Voice as if from Heaven's depths;
They cast their eyes about in wonderment,
For none could understand the meaning of
Celestial tones to mortal ears downsent.
Again the Voice rolled forth—nor harsh nor loud,
Though piercing in its mild simplicity,
That every breast be caused to quake, each heart
To burn, and every Soul to yearn for Light,
For Truth, for God. A third time came the Voice;
And auditors terrestrial up-looked
Steadfastly toward Deep Heaven from whence it came,
Until at last they understood the Words:
*"Behold, behold my Lovéd Son, in Whom
I glorify My Name*—Hear ye Him*!"*
    And it came to pass that as they understood,
The People looked again toward the Sound
And saw a Man aureolate descend,
Clothed in white, majestic, pure, divine,
Robed in glory, suffused with living Light.
He came to them and stood before wide doors
That opened on the Temple's Sanctity;
And in the shadows of His Holy House
(Though where He was no shadows spread their pall,
For Light was all in all, through all, with all,
So glowing and so Light His Countenance),
Stretched He His Hands toward the multitude,
Smiling graciously as He thus spake:
    "Behold, *I am Jesus Christ,* whom Prophets
Testified should come unto the World.
I am the Light and Life of Mortal Spheres,

Of Worlds unnumbered though to the Father known.
I have drunk deeply of the bitter Cup
Which the Father proffered me, and have glorified
The Father's Name eternally; for I
Have now assumed all worlds' sinful shames,
Have suffered the Father's Will in Death and Life."
    At this the multitude on knee bowed low
In witness of *Theophany* supreme,
Remembering the Prophecies divine
That One should come who was God's only Son,
Who should revealéd be in glorious state,
The One begotten of All-Father's Flesh
And Flesh and Blood transform to Flesh and Bone;
And as the Risen Lord invited all
To come and touch deep prints of cruel spikes
Participant in fearful *Deicide*,
And thrust their hands into His wounded Side
Where *Cæsar*'s lance caused precious Blood to flow,
Sanguinary tears for Humanity's grave sins,
Bloody tears for Humans' conscious sins,
With purest Water painfully conjoined;
Yea, as the Risen Lord invited all to come,
Young Nephi felt his muscles tight-constrict,
And seemed to step into the multitude,
Toward his beatific Vision of
The Resurrected *Christ,* the Son of God.
Yet could he not, for firm upon his arm
An unseen hand was lain, restraining him
As souls redeemed with reverence approached
The God who suffered Justice's firm decree
To bring about through Mercy and high Love
Satisfaction of the exigencies
By Adam's Fall upon all flesh impelled.
    In consternation deep, bold Nephi turned,
Perceiving none yet feeling hindrance sure,
Prohibiting participation in
The sacred scene before him surely set;

And as he sought the source of Powers unseen
The multitudes surrounding him dispelled,
His glorious Vision of the *Christ* grew dim—
Nephi struggled to retain the form
Of Heaven's *Anointed One* within his mind,
While men corporeal (as Autumn mists
Beneath the flames of latent Summer's sun
First dimming, or industrious bees with
Communal hum grow from a distance vague,
Indistinct) merged into Eternity,
Leaving Lehi's son beside raised stones,
An Altar firm upon a desert Mount.
    He was alone. White stones no longer glowed
With Light Celestial; and as the youth
With pensive heart in meditative still
Down-knelt amid slight, cool, refreshing winds,
The Voice of *Him Who was to Come* arose,
And comfort flowed with unrestrained force
Into full Being in the beardless one:
"This Vision I have shown thee, son of man,
That thou might know the purpose for thy Act.
The Plates, for which thou slew'st a Kinsman cruel,
Are indispensable unto thy Seed;
This much thou know'st, for thus hast thou beheld
Thy People's History until the Time
In time's Meridian when all shall fail
That leads not to just Life and Heaven's Joys.
    "Much of what thou hast this night perceived
Shalt thou indite upon thy sacred Plates,
Which Chronicle one day shall set my Truths
Renewed into the breasts of erring men;
But not yet all, for of thy Father's troop
Are none now ripe to share bright Truths entire
Which thou has seen. Other Prophet-Seers,
In other times, shall also see these things
And theirs the Office is to publish them
Unto the waiting hearts of men prepared.

Now rest, my Child. Return unto the Camp
Of Lehi's wandering age, and sleep content.
Thy Faith is tried and proven, this Task fulfilled.
All that thou didst shall benefit thy Seed,
And they in righteousness shall sing high Praise
To their obedient Progenitor."
    And with these closing syllables divine,
Voice and Vision ceased; and in the East,
Scarce one hand's breadth above the World's rim,
A Stellar Beacon—sun unto an Earth
Created, saved, and loved by Him who set
Our turquoise-emerald Sphere upon its course
Through vast immensities of Space and Time—
This Stellar Beacon shed clear, crystal Light
Upon a youthful Prophet's chosen Path;
Toward great Lehi's night-excluding tents,
And thence beyond, into a Promised Land.

AUTHOR'S AFTERWORD

TO THE 1996 EDITION

A word of explanation...and a *caveat*.

The Nephiad unabashedly imitates a form long past its prime of popularity, possibly even of readability. Seventeenth-Century *Iadic* Epic—with its panoply of conventions ranging from the archaic to the exotic; its conscious (at times self-conscious) elevation of diction and tone, subject and style; its attempt to express an encyclopedic knowledge of the poet's world; its persistent demand that the reader bring nearly as much energy to the work as the poet—this form of Epic barely survived Milton's culminating efforts in *Paradise Lost* and *Paradise Regained*. Indeed, in spite of frequent Miltonic imitations, almost all of limited durability and even more limited success, poets struggled for the next two hundred years to find a way to breathe new life into the ancient form, a struggle resulting in works such as Tennyson's *Idylls of the King*; David Jones's *In Parenthesis* and *The Anathémata*; T. S. Eliot's anti-epical *The Waste Land*; William Carlos William's *Paterson*; Charles Williams's *Taliessin Through Logres*; J. R. R. Tolkien's *The Lord of the Rings*; Frank Herbert's *Dune*; Stephen King's *The Stand*; and uncounted other works of prose and poetry as diverse and as exciting as these.

To write a Renaissance-styled *Nephiad,* then, was an act of willfulness on my part. Knowing full well that most modern readers would find the form archaic, stilted, convoluted (both necessarily and, perhaps, unnecessarily), I nonetheless tried, over the course of more than twenty years, to understand as much as possible of what Milton had attempted and achieved, and to incorporate what I could of that success into my own poem.

The Nephiad began as a simple exercise: After all, what better way for a graduate student immersed in Milton studies to understand the intricacies of Milton's poem, or the particular decisions Milton made at every moment in *Paradise Lost,* than by trying to re-create the impetus that led to each? At a time when I should, perhaps, have concentrated on preparing for examinations and on writing my dissertation (not coincidentally focusing on Milton and Moral Agency), I struggled through the first version of this poem—only to discover that it had rapidly ceased being a simple exercise and became something far more important—to me at least.

After two decades that include multiple opportunities to teach Milton, Seventeenth-Century Poetry, Epic Theory, and Creative Writing, I have returned to that first draft and completed it, bringing my own years of apprenticeship to bear on this single, long attempt at Epic.

And now, the *caveat.*

The Nephiad is, for all its strengths and/or failings, for all the ambition of form and length and content, merely a *poem.* It pretends to be neither history nor theology; and where it diverges from either, it represents strictly artistic decisions, not attempts to re-write *Book of Mormon* history or claims to speak for God. I am aware of elements in the poem that may strike my readers (if there have been any brave enough to tackle the sheer bulk of what is offered) as distorted or unusual. These are my contributions and are not to be taken as criticisms, emendations, or adjuncts to scripture.

My gratitude to many people who helped bring *The Nephiad* to fruition, but particularly to Professor John M. Steadman for his invaluable insights into all things Miltonic; to Orson Scott Card for the challenge and the impetus (and his position on the relative merits of Spenser and Milton); to Satya Elizabeth Gratner (who *is* White Crow Press) for her enthusiasm for poetry and poetry-books; and, as always, to Judith, who bears with more than Christian patience and fortitude my frequent forays into poetry.

—**Michael R. Collings**

ABOUT THE AUTHOR

MICHAEL R. COLLINGS is an Emeritus Professor of English at Pepperdine University and the author of over thirty volumes of poetry, novels, short fiction, bibliography, and studies of writers including Stephen King, Dean R. Koontz, Piers Anthony, Brian W. Aldiss, and Orson Scott Card. Many of his books have been published by the Borgo Press Imprint of Wildside Press, his most recent being *The Art and Craft of Poetry* and the science-fiction novel, *Singer of Lies*. He lives and works in Idaho.

www.ingramcontent.com/pod-product-compliance
Lightning Source LLC
LaVergne TN
LVHW041618070426
835507LV00008B/321